David Daube

Appeasement or Resistance

and Other Essays on
New Testament Judaism

University of California Press
Berkeley   Los Angeles   London

University of California Press
Berkeley and Los Angeles, California

University of California Press, Ltd.
London, England

© 1987 by
The Regents of the University of California

Library of Congress Cataloging-in-Publication Data

Daube, David.
  Appeasement or resistance and other essays on
New Testament Judaism.
  Includes index.
  1. Bible. N.T.—Relation to the Old Testament.
2. Government, Resistance to—Biblical teaching.
3. Bible. N.T.—Criticism, interpretation, etc.
I. Title.
BS2387.D38   1987   225.6   87-12462
ISBN 0-520-06158-6 (alk. paper)

Printed in the United States of America
1 2 3 4 5 6 7 8 9

Contents

The Old Testament in the New: A Jewish
   Perspective   1

Temple Tax   39

The Burdened Convert   59

Appeasing or Resisting the Oppressor   75

   Index of Passages Cited   121

The Old Testament in the New: A Jewish Perspective

I.   Outline

The New Testament frequently cites the Old, from centuries before. Now whenever people base on an ancient text, for a comprehension of their drift it matters little what that text means or, to put it more humbly, what we suppose it to mean; the key lies in what it means to them, which may be quite different. To some extent, this is true even where the text is contemporaneous. Say, you form an opinion or take action inspired by an item in today's *San Francisco Chronicle*. If it is you I am out to understand, I must concentrate not on what the article says but on what it says to you. Even in such a case, the discrepancy now and

An expanded version of the George Hitchings Terriberry Memorial Lecture delivered at Newcomb College, Tulane University, on October 26, 1982. I dedicate it in gratitude to my friend David Patterson and his family. Nineteen eighty-two was the year when his admirers around the world celebrated his sixtieth birthday. A German translation by Wolfgang Schuller has appeared as volume 10, 1984, of the series *Xenia* which he edits.

then will be enormous. However, the likelihood of its being so is less.

Here is an example unrelated to the Bible. To make sense of the itineraries chosen in the age of Columbus by the seekers of Atlantis, the lost island figuring in the Arabian geographers, we must proceed not from where the latter place it but from where the Renaissance voyagers believed they did. Next, for a complaint about the Old Testament by Hamlet, who wishes God had promulgated no law against suicide. Shakespeare has in mind 'Thou shalt not murder', assumed in his time to extend to self-killing.[1] Few scholars nowadays go along with this range of the commandment but, as far as an appreciation of the monologue in question is concerned, this is beside the point. Noah's three sons offer further illustrations. Dutch Reformed churchmen in South Africa, in defence of racial oppression, adduce his curse dubbing Ham–Canaan a servant of servants to Shem and Japheth.[2] Fairly logical, given their view that from the one wicked brother are descended the present blacks and from the decent pair of Shem and Japheth the present whites, that the pronouncement is designed to punish all the former and reward all the latter, and so forth. The craziness of their view does not make it any less the explanation of their reliance on this passage. In the first half of the second century A.D., Simon ben Gamaliel II, permitting the writing of the Torah in Greek, appeals to another portion of Noah's oracle: 'Japheth shall dwell in the tents of Shem'.[3] The force of the quotation emerges when we remember that, for the Rabbis, Japheth stood for Hellas and

1. Shakespeare, *Hamlet*, 1.2.132, Exodus 20.13, Deuteronomy 5.17.
2. Genesis 9.25.
3. Palestinian Megillah 71c, Genesis 9.26.

Shem for Jewry. To follow Simon, it is this that we need to know, while how far the identifications coincide with the original meaning is of secondary interest.[4]

My proposition, then—far from novel but too readily neglected—is that, when dealing with the Old Testament in the New, we ought to read it as it was read by the Jews of that era. The references without exception come from their midst, are founded on their interpretation. If this often clashes with the pristine sense (or what we take to be such) it cannot be helped. We must still stick to it. Unless we do, we may miss parts—from relatively minor to very major— of the New Testament message conveyed by means of the reference.

In passing, the chief reason for the widespread disregard of this strategy is that it requires being steeped in the Rabbinic modes of exegesis, and few Christian theologians are. The most excellent collections of Talmudic material bearing on the New Testament cannot fully make up for this shortcoming. Luckily, owing to a variety of factors—one of them, the discovery of the Dead Sea Scrolls—the situation is improving; and at least the number of those explicitly minimizing the importance of what went on among the Jews of the period seems in decline. But I have no illusions. As we know from the fable of the fox and the grapes, to pooh-pooh what we cannot tackle is a natural—and, up to a point, healthy—defence mechanism. I have confessed

4. Jan Vetter, when I told him of this essay, drew my attention to a 1977 Supreme Court decision in *St. Paul Fire and Marine Insurance Co.* v. *Barry*, written by Powell J. and approving of a remark by Mr. Justice Cardozo in 1935, that 'words or phrases in a statute come freighted with the meaning imparted to them by the mischief to be remedied and by contemporaneous discussion. In such conditions history is a teacher that is not to be ignored'. I am grateful to Walter Pakter for helping me locate these opinions.

elsewhere that when, some time ago, a colleague from Sofia sent me his manual on Roman law, in Bulgarian, I laid it aside, comforting myself with the thought that it was unlikely to contain much that was radically new.

II.   God of Our Fathers

Perhaps I had best begin with a quotation most scholars do treat as distorting the genuine tenor, Rabbi-wise: a clause from the Book of Exodus which Jesus thinks confirms resurrection.[1] More carefully, is represented as thinking; but I shall submit grounds for crediting the report. The reason the incongruity in this instance is widely admitted is that the ratiocination, the 'logic'—fancy to us—turning the clause into a proof of resurrection, is offered in full.

Resurrection, a fundamental tenet of the Pharisees, is nowhere mentioned in the Pentateuch—to their grave embarrassment vis-à-vis Samaritans and Sadducees for whom Mosaic directives alone were binding and who rejected this dogma of later provenance. Its upholders, in consequence, were driven to all sorts of twistings of holy writ to convict their opponents of error even by their own standard. For example, Deuteronomy speaks of 'the land which the Lord swore to your Fathers to give to them and to their seed'. But, the Pharisees argued, the Fathers died before their seed reached Canaan; how, then, could God give the land to them as well as to the latter? Answer: because they will return. Mosaic evidence.[2] It was taken seriously enough for the Samaritans to excise 'to them' from their version. Nor

---

1. Matthew 22.31f., Mark 12.26f., Luke 20.37f., Exodus 3.6.
2. Babylonian Sanhedrin 90b, Deuteronomy 11.9, 21.

must they be labelled as fraudulent.[3] They believed they
were throwing out an intrusion no less honestly than the
Pharisaic masters believed they were uncovering its true
contents. The same Gamaliel II in whose name this proof is
transmitted, as well as his contemporary Joshua ben Hananiah—around A.D. 100—made use of a grammar-defying
method to produce further testimony. Towards the close of
Deuteronomy, God tells Moses: 'You will be resting with
your Fathers, and there will be rising this people and be
whoring after the gods of the strangers'. The two asserted
that 'and there will be rising' attached to both the preceding part and the following part, so we obtain (1) 'you will
be resting with your Fathers and there will be rising'—resurrection, (2) 'and there will be rising this people and be
whoring'—Israel's lapse.[4]

Jesus confronts the Sadducees with God's self-revelation
to Moses: 'I am the God of Abraham, the God of Isaac and
the God of Jacob'. The incident takes place long after the
days of the Patriarchs. But plainly, Jesus argues, God must
be a God of the living. It follows that they are not departed
for ever: they will come back. Mosaic evidence of the same
character as Gamaliel's.[5] To do justice to the New Testament

3. As they are by Eliezer ben Jose, around A.D. 150, in
Babylonian Sanhedrin 90b. For further details, see my comments
in *Jewish Journal of Sociology* 3 (1961): 23.

4. Babylonian Sanhedrin 90b, Deuteronomy 31.16. The
method is discussed by me in *Festschrift Hans Lewald*, 1953,
pp. 34ff. Classical specimens reached the Elizabethans and, if
B. Everett, writing in the *London Review of Books*, 18 December
1986, p. 7, is right, 'wisheth' in the dedication of Shakespeare's
Sonnets faces in two directions.

5. Virtually conceded on all hands. Still, not a few authorities, believing Jesus to be the originator of this proof, are at pains
to elevate it. Thus, K. H. Rengstorf, *Das Evangelium nach Lukas*,

sense of the line, no use looking at it from the standpoint of the composer of Exodus; we have to put on Rabbinic spectacles.

This is all that is essential to my thesis. The subject matter is of such weight, however, as to deserve an excursus.

That Jesus invented the syllogism is a priori implausible, surely. Fortunately, it can be shown that he did not. It definitely underlies, for example, the doctrine of IV Maccabees, on which a little more presently; and almost certainly the proofs from Deuteronomy—also with the Fathers in a prototypal role—are offshoots, weaker than the model 'I am the God of' etc. which centers on the very opening of the Almighty's decisive intervention in Exodus. It is demonstrable, too, that one had to be no academic to be acquainted with it: that is why I have no qualms as to historicity. It was in fact by his time deeply embedded in the central daily prayer, the Eighteen Benedictions.

As pointed out by Herbert Loewe (in whose home I had my first meal at Cambridge in the thirties), when the Sadducees are declared in this debate 'to know neither the Scriptures nor the power of God', the latter term denotes the Second Benediction, aimed against them and carrying the appellation 'Powers'.[6] The First Benediction, with the appellation 'Fathers', addresses 'the God of Abraham, the God of Isaac and the God of Jacob'—from the Book of

---

9th ed., 1962, p. 229, greatly refines its message, while E. Klostermann, *Das Markusevangelium*, 4th ed., 1950, deems it *geistreicher*, 'more ingenious', than the ordinary run.

6. See C. G. Montefiore and H. Loewe, *A Rabbinic Anthology*, 1938; rept. with prolegomenon by R. Loewe, 1974, p. 369. The idea is taken up by R. Loewe, *Journal of Theological Studies*, n.s. 32 (1981): 358. But he assumes that the evangelists are no longer aware of Jesus's meaning—which, at least as far as Mark is concerned, seems unwarranted.

Exodus. The Second extols him as 'powerful' and 'Lord of powers' in reviving the dead and also, significantly, as the giver of rain.[7] Clearly, the sequence is determined by that notion that the formulation in Exodus guarantees resurrection. Whether this Benediction was coined in its entirety during the fierce struggles between the sects in the second century B.C. or whether, as has been suggested, the bulk of it dates from before and only the contested principle was inserted in that period, we may leave open. Here, by the time of Jesus, was the Pharisaic case, accessible to everybody. The Sadducees, he is saying, ignore a vital teaching of the Torah, as explicated in the Second Benediction. Luke has cut out this somewhat parochial reprimand, preserved in Matthew and Mark.[8]

Various considerations supporting this approach may be

7. Cf. Isaiah 26.19. I shall return to the mention of rain at the end of II.

8. Here is a translation (which, sorry to say, does not convey the beauty, strength and depth of the Hebrew): Blessed are you, O Lord our God and God of our Fathers, God of Abraham, God of Isaac and God of Jacob, great, powerful and awesome God, God the Highest, who bestows beneficent kindnesses and possesses all and remembers the kindnesses of the Fathers and brings a redeemer to their children's children for his name's sake in love; King, Helper and Saviour and Shield; Blessed are you, O Lord, the Shield of Abraham. —Second Benediction: You are powerful for ever, O Lord, who revives the dead, you are mighty to save; who causes the wind to blow and the rain to descend; who sustains the living in kindness, who revives the dead with much mercy, who supports the falling and heals the sick and looses the bound and keeps his faith to those sleeping in the dust; who is like you, O Lord of powers, and who resembles you? King who kills and revives and causes salvation to spring forth; and faithful you are to revive the dead; Blessed are you, O Lord, who revives the dead.

added. For a start, let me dispose of a possible objection: Jesus employs the singular, 'power of God', the Talmud the plural, 'Powers'. Not a serious stumbling block. The plural embraces the several powers appearing in the Benediction—resurrection, rain, provision of good, healing, salvation, even killing—while Jesus concentrates on the first. There is plenty of evidence that singular and plural are not kept rigidly separate in this province, and no doubt the earlier the date, the more fluidity. In the third century still, the question why, traditionally, one speaks of 'powers of rains' in discussing the Second Benediction, is answered: 'Because they come down by the power [of God]'.[9]

Now for a more positive input. It was usual then to cite important divisions of sacred works by means of conventional, pregnant designations. As it happens, Jesus on the same occasion avails himself of this mode not only for the Second Benediction, 'Powers', but also for the verse from Exodus: 'Have you not read in the Book of Moses, at the Bush'. 'The Bush' figures in Rabbinic material as the appellation of the pericope recounting God's first appearance to Moses.[10] In this case, Matthew—against Mark and Luke—has dropped the technical detail, along with 'the Book of Moses', to replace it by his favourite 'that which is said'.[11]

To go by Mark, throughout the debate, both Sadducees and Jesus speak of 'a rising' (noun) or 'to rise' (verb); once

9. Johanan bar Nappaha in Babylonian Taanith 2a.

10. See H. L. Strack and P. Billerbeck, *Kommentar zum Neuen Testament aus Talmud und Midrasch*, 4 vols., 1924–1929, rept. 1969, 2:28.

11. To disentangle the various New Testament writers' systems of citation cannot be my task here. I am content to observe that 'that which is said' or 'it has been said' is never met in Mark and that whenever Matthew puts it without specifying the source, he is citing the Pentateuch.

only, in interpreting 'I am the God of' etc., he substitutes the dead 'being waked'. Some scholars who have noticed the switch justly attribute it to the idea, well attested in the Talmud, of death as not final annihilation but temporary sleep. The Fathers are alive, just sleeping, waiting to be re-summoned.[12] According to IV Maccabees, the martyrs are convinced that 'unto God, they die not, as our Fathers Abraham, Isaac and Jacob died not, but that they live unto God'.[13] In the Qumran hymns, at Judgment time, 'all the sons of his truth will awake' and 'those that rest in the dust' will hoist the banner.[14] What is significant for us is that the so-called Babylonian rescension of the Second Benediction (so-called—it seems to be a product of Palestine just as much as the Palestinian version)[15] explicitly glorifies God as 'keeping his faith to them that sleep in the dust'. Indeed, it borrows the image from the Book of Daniel where we also meet the verb 'to awake': 'And many of them that sleep in the dust of the earth shall awake'.[16]

The famous pronouncement in I Corinthians 15 stands foursquare in this tradition: 'Some of them [that saw Christ after his burial] are fallen asleep', 'Christ has been awakened from the dead, the first-fruits of them that slept', 'we shall not all sleep'.[17] Nor is the key word 'power' missing: 'Sown in weakness, awakened in [or by] power'.[18] Of the many other contributions—direct or indirect—to this concern, some concur, some deviate, slightly or markedly. It is a

12. See Klostermann, *Markusevangelium*, pp. 126, 180.
13. IV Maccabees 7.19, similarly 16.25. This is not to affirm absolute identity with the attitude of Jesus.
14. I Qumran Hodayoth 6.29f., 34.
15. See Strack and Billerbeck, *Kommentar*, 4, pt. 1: 211.
16. Daniel 12.2.
17. I Corinthians 15.6, 20, 51.
18. I Corinthians 15.43; cf. 6.14, II Corinthians 13.4.

quest touching on the most diverse facets of the infant Church.

English translations, not excepting the most meticulous ones, as a rule put 'to rise' or 'to raise' even where the Greek has 'to be awakened' or 'to awake' (transitive). One cause—repeat: one of a dozen—is surely the far greater convenience of the former pair; my parenthesis (transitive) illustrates a drawback of the latter. In German, there is no awkwardness about *auferweckt werden* or *auferwecken*, hence these two are fairly frequent. Actually, German has some difficulty with 'to raise': *auferstehen lassen* is clumsy. So in German renderings, it is this term which is apt to be pushed out—by *auferwecken*.[19] Admittedly, the mix-up is provided with a justification—to wit, that, in Greek literature, 'to be awakened' not seldom has the sense of 'to rise' and 'to awaken' (transitive) that of 'to raise'. However, this happens only in special conditions and a metaphorical flavour nearly always persists. As for the New Testament, though here and there synonymity of the two verbs is reached, in the vast majority of cases it is not, small as the difference may at times be. It is wrong to postulate that the adoption of the noun *anastasis*, 'resurrection', 'rising', as the chief heading in this domain spells the end of nuances. Roughly, 'to be awakened' and 'to awake' do remain narrower, evoke a definite mode of coming back. A friend of mine has enrolled in a class on 'cooking' in order to learn 'to bake'. Furthermore, quite apart from any substantive distinction, the verb opted for almost invariably points to a certain historical filiation—which, indeed, can still influence the mood, the aura, of a passage. Helen often uses 'to block out' or 'to repress' instead of my pedestrian 'to forget'. She has long given up the axiom that any lapse of memory is due to unwillingness to remember. So the for-

19. E.g. Acts 2.24.

mer verbs continue (1) meaningfully, in a few situations where she does assume such a mechanism, (2) as a habit of speech, where it may or may not be at work or even, on occasion, where it most probably is not. No matter what the circumstances, her idiom links her historically to a movement to which I, belonging to an earlier generation and growing up in good, old Freiburg, was not exposed in my formative years. Moral: even where 'rising' and 'awaking' are equivalent, the choice of one or the other will very likely be a clue to antecedents of the statement.

Once in process, the painting out of shades goes on and on. 'Some of them are fallen asleep' etc., adverted to above, in the New English Bible and Anchor Bible runs 'some have died', 'the first-fruits of them that have died', 'we shall not all die'. Standardization. I shall not heap excursus on excursus to document my claim but be content with remarking that the trend is demonstrable from very early on. A fragment from the Gospel according to the Hebrews, preserved in Latin by Jerome, has James vow at the end of the Last Supper that he will not eat till he sees Jesus 'rise from the sleeping', and Jesus, returned from the grave, breaks bread, hands him a piece and assures him that he has indeed 'risen from the sleeping': *resurgere a dormientibus*.[20] The Greek translation of Jerome gives us 'from the dead', *ek nekron*, and in Latin writers using Jerome we also come across *a mortuis*. Curiously, whereas Jerome twice speaks of 'to rise', *resurgere*, the Greek version puts *anistamai* only the first time and then goes over to 'to be awakened', *egeiro*. The impact of *a dormientibus*, it appears, was strong enough to evoke this image in the translator even though he gave up 'to sleep' in favour of the less specific 'dead'.

20. The Gospel according to the Hebrews 8, from Jerome, *De Viris Illustribus* 2. On a different aspect of the passage, see my *Wine in the Bible*, 1974, p. 14.

I submit that if, for an experimental period of twenty years, scholars Englished, Germaned, Frenched etc. the texts in strict compliance with the Greek, it would lead to worthwhile results. Nabakov, I am confident, would have backed me. Far be it from me to recommend this pedantry for Bible lovers not engaged in research. Take Jesus's forecast in John that he will 'awaken' the destroyed temple in three days, thinking of his body.[21] Any popular edition must substitute something like 'rebuild'. Yet scholars even here ought not to slur over the evangelist's selection. I am aware that *egeiro* can denote 'to erect a building' without any allusion to sleep. In fact, it may have been commoner in this sense than one might suppose from extant evidence: the corresponding Latin *excito*, met in Cicero and Caesar, is, I guess, an imitation. (The Vulgate avails itself of it in this pericope.) Nevertheless, it is decidedly not the most obvious verb in the field. John, in preferring it, conveys a particular notion of resurrection. As for 'to die' in lieu of 'to fall asleep', perhaps a modern audience likes the blunter word. I would have thought that 'first-fruits' was more antiquated. Gretchen's brother, in Goethe's *Faust*,[22] let us note, conceives of death as a sleep to end (at least for the just ones) by being allowed into the presence of God: *Ich gehe durch den Todesschlaf zu Gott ein als Soldat und brav*, 'I go in to God, through the sleep of death, as a soldier and a good fellow'.

It is just conceivable that even Jesus's portrayal of the risen ones as of the nature of angels falls within the orbit of the Eighteen Benedictions. A number of Jewish parallels have been collected; those in Enoch particularly impressive[23]

21. John 2.19ff.

22. Goethe, *Faust*, Part One, Scene: Street in front of Gretchen's house.

23. See Strack and Billerbeck, *Kommentar*, 1:891.

since this corpus was influential at the very inception of Christianity. Here I have in mind the Third Benediction, 'Sanctification', which at least when recited in public includes the Thrice-Holy of Isaiah's seraphim.[24] The earthly community, that is, after 'Fathers' and 'Powers', worships in the manner of the celestial one—maybe in anticipation of the ultimate transfiguration. The first Three Benedictions, it is worth recalling, were seen as belonging together, devoted to praise, the subsequent clusters being petitions and thanks.[25] The implication: the first three do not ask God to exert his might and mercy but acknowledge him as possessed of them.[26]

A few thoughts about Acts. Twice we find Peter and his companions proclaim that 'the God of Abraham, Isaac and

24. Isaiah 6.3. Translation: We will sanctify your name in the world as they sanctify it in the heavens above, as it is written by the hand of your prophet, And they called one to the other and said, Holy, holy, holy is the Lord of Hosts, the whole earth is full of his glory; those over against them would say Blessed; Blessed is the glory of the Lord from his place; and in your Holy Words it is written, saying, The Lord shall reign for ever, your God, O Zion, from generation to generation, Praise the Lord; from generation to generation we will proclaim your greatness and to the eternity of eternities your Holiness we will sanctify, and your exaltation shall not depart from our mouth for ever and ever, for a great and holy God and King you are; Blessed are you, O Lord, the Holy God.

25. See Strack and Billerbeck, *Kommentar*, 4, pt. 1: 214ff. The petitions are for Understanding, Repentance, Forgiveness and so on, the thanks for benefactions throughout the ages and in the present.

26. Oh that we had been spared the Freudians. Today, when your wife compliments you, 'You are sweeter than any of the five hubbies I have had before', you suspect that she wants something special.

Jacob' or 'the God of our Fathers' has awakened Jesus[27]—
doubtless harking back to the stand Jesus took when as-
sailed by the Sadducees. That episode, it will be remem-
bered, is incorporated in all Synoptic Gospels, including
that of Luke, author of Acts. Jesus, the choice of language is
conveying, placed his trust in the assurance enshrined in
this particular self-revelation of God; and the God who had
thus revealed himself did prove him right and restore him
to eternal life.

In a subsequent section, focusing on Paul, we hear of the
Sadducees averring 'that there is no resurrection neither angel nor spirit'.[28] It is universally agreed that this represents
them as dismissing angelology. One half of the literature
accepts the allegation though it is corroborated in not a
single other source and though angels are accredited by the
Pentateuch. The other half assumes a blunder, though how
that could occur on a topic of such popular interest is hard
to imagine. In actual fact, the statement has to do not with
angelology as a whole but with the Jesuanic concept of the
risen ones as akin to angels. 'Resurrection and angel' equals
'rising and donning an angel's existence'. It is this peculiar
species of angel the Sadducees deny—which, indeed,
shows them fully at ease with angelology as such. The dis-
sension between Pharisees and Sadducees depicted in this
chapter is stirred up by Paul in order to get the former on
his side: he protests that those who raged against his sermon on the previous day did so because it expressed faith in
resurrection. Perfectly true, no deception: already in the
preceding portion about Peter and John, just inspected, we
learn that the Sadducees resented 'their preaching through
Jesus the resurrection of the dead'.[29] At any rate, no need

27. Acts 3.13ff., 5.30.   28. Acts 23.8.
29. Acts 4.2.

whatever for the narrator to drag in angelology in general, while a reminder of the superior understanding of resurrection, by disclosing which Jesus repulsed the Sadducees, is highly appropriate.

There is yet a bit more to it. Remarkable stress is laid in this account on Pharisaic approval of his concept: 'the Pharisees confess both',[30] i.e., not only resurrection but also radical transmutation. Tying in with the concession by some of their scribes that 'if a spirit or angel has spoken to him . . .'.[31] Once more, by no means a reference to angels at large. It takes up exclusively the two visions of the risen Jesus detailed by Paul the day before, the first of them in light so overwhelming that no earthly being could dwell in it unblinded.[32] That this momentous aspect of his experience, a direct manifestation of the wholly different make-up of the new body—'we shall be changed' in I Corinthians[33]—should have an impact on his listeners is scarcely surprising. But there is absolutely no indication of the scribes going on to wider, unconnected questions. It looks to me as if a rare, specific contact between Acts and the Third Gospel might now gain in import. As in Matthew and Mark, so in Luke, Jesus's view of resurrection obtains Pharisaic assent, but in Luke alone it comes from 'certain of the scribes'—the same phrasing as in Acts.[34] We may well be moving in the realm of prefiguring and re-enacting.

It may be asked why, whereas Jesus likened the risen

---

30. Acts 23.8.   31. Acts 23.9.   32. Acts 22.6ff.
33. I Corinthians 15.51.

34. This is wholly compatible with the view of J. M. Creed, *The Gospel According to St. Luke*, 1930, p. 250, that the verse has been suggested by Mark 12.28. What is of interest here is precisely the subtle deviation from the latter in position and formulation.

ones to angels, in Acts it is 'angel or spirit' or 'spirit or angel'. 'Spirit' would be a legitimate accommodation to an
educated public of the period.[35] It alone figures in I Corinthians 15. Also towards the end of Luke, where Jesus, risen
from the grave but not yet carried up into heaven, still has
flesh and bones—in contradistinction to 'a spirit'.[36] ('A
ghost'—even in the New English Bible—is sadly mislead-
ing and, indeed, vulgarizing.[37] It would be—significantly—
an acceptable rendering of *eidolon* in a scene from *The Life
of Apollonius*.[38]) In Romans 8, there is much to and fro[39] between God's or Christ's life-giving 'Spirit' and the Christian raised by it to become 'spirit'. Which enables me to
end with the bee in my bonnet. Hebrew *ruah*, 'breath',
'wind', 'spirit', has life-giving force in a clause of the Second Benediction briefly introduced towards the beginning
of this discussion. During the months between the Feast of
Tabernacles and that of Passover, there is inserted into this
Benediction the acknowledgment of God as 'causing the
wind to blow and the rain to fall'.

---

35. The chapter on Lord of the Spirit in W. D. Davies, *Paul
and Rabbinic Judaism*, 1948, rept. 1958, pp. 177ff., is invaluable for
this and related problems.

36. Luke 24.37, 39.

37. So is Rengstorf's treatment of the scene, *Evangelium nach
Lukas*, p. 285, as analogous to the Walking on the Water in Matthew 24.22ff., Mark 6.45ff.—where we hear not of *pneuma* at all
but of *phantasma*. Creed, *Gospel According to Luke*, p. 298f., does
not bring in that incident.

38. Philostratus, *The Life of Apollonius of Tyana* 8.12 towards
the beginning.

39. Sensitively annotated by C. H. Dodd, *The Epistle of Paul
to the Romans*, 1932, pp. 116ff.

III.   Male and Female

According to Matthew and Mark, the Pharisees question Jesus concerning divorce, in the hope of cornering him:[1] they know that he is opposed but, should he say so, he will be spurning the law of Deuteronomy where it is permitted. Jesus triumphs by showing that Scripture itself, in two texts, classes that law as a *pis aller*, tailored to a depraved people. My main business is with the first, which to begin with certainly stood alone: 'Male and female created he them'.[2]

Why ever should this have borne him out? So God made two species: does this impose an indissoluble bond? From the plain wording, the contrary inference would be almost more plausible. In Isaiah, God speaks of himself as 'making peace and creating evil'.[3] One would not deduce that an irenic person ought never to give up vice.

The solution lies in the then cherished, esoteric teaching, preserved in Midrash and Philo,[4] that the verse envisages the *Ur*-Adam, androgynous, male and female in one. A variant of the Septuagint mentioned by the Rabbis in fact rendered it: 'Male and female genitals of his created he him'. Obviously, taken thus, it is a tremendous weapon against divorce, as also, let us note, against polygamy. The

1.   Matthew 19.3ff., Mark 10.2ff. See my *The New Testament and Rabbinic Judaism*, 1956, rept. 1973, pp. 71ff., and my oration in *Journal of Jewish Studies* 10 (1959): 1ff. A similar attempt will be inspected below, under VII.

2.   Genesis 1.27, 5.2.

3.   Isaiah 45.7.

4.   Genesis Rabba on 1.26f., Mekhilta on Exodus 12.40, Philo, *On the Creation* 24.76, *Allegorical Interpretation of the Laws* 2.4.13, *Who Is the Heir* 33.164.

first human, formed in the image of God, constituted a
lasting union of the two sexes. The Zadokite Fragments, in
combating polygamy and divorce, give pride of place to
this very line, calling it 'a fundamental principle of the creation'.[5] Just so, Jesus demands that this ideal 'from the beginning of the creation' guide the community now starting
out afresh. In my opinion, at one time, the conclusion fol-
lowed immediately on this first text: 'What therefore God
has joined together, let not man put asunder'—the creature
may not dare disdain the pattern set up by the creator.

How the exegetes came to peg the androgynous shape of
the pristine Adam onto this specific verse I have explained
elsewhere.[6] Their doctrine, of course, is reminiscent of Ar-
istophanes's in Plato's *Symposium*.[7] My hunch is that its core
hails from the Orient. The Greeks took it over, like many
other myths, and elaborated it in their way—achieving a
brilliant complexity. Jewish probers into the divine scheme
must have found the idea alluring as soon as they reflected
deeply on that Adam from whose side God removed Eve;
which does not exclude the possibility of their speculations
being refertilized by Greek ones in the Hellenistic epoch.

The second text, culminating in 'and the twain shall be
one flesh', looks far more to the point;[8] indeed, it is its
presence which has, so to speak, carried the first, saved it
from being a puzzle. It, too, however, as I have tried to
show, in the mind of whoever originally affixed it—Jesus
himself or an early expositor—exhorts a mankind not yet
perverted to aspire to that initial wholeness. This, irrespective of what we may deem the authentic drift in Genesis,

5. Zadokite Fragments 7.1ff.
6. See the works cited in footnote 1.
7. Plato, *Symposium* 189C ff.
8. Genesis 2.24.

gives it its special force in Mark—though probably no longer in Matthew, but I shall not pursue this change.

Why was it added? Because the first text was an argument from example—how God fashioned the world. But the Pharisaic leaders more and more insisted that, in putting forward binding regulations, you must argue from precept. 'The two shall be one flesh' had the requisite style. The Zadokite Fragments contain three quotations. The first two, examples: 'Male and female created he them' and 'The animals went in two by two'. The third—definitely a supplement—a precept: 'The king shall not multiply wives to himself'.[9]

IV.   Eye for Eye

The Sermon on the Mount opposes to the maxim 'eye for eye' and so on non-resistance and turning the other cheek.[1] Commentators, oblivious of the amazing change in meaning an Old Testament rule might undergo in the course of a thousand years or so, think of an attack on physical talion.[2] However, this practice had long disappeared; not one in-

---

9. Genesis 1.27, 5.2, 7.9, Deuteronomy 17.17.

1. Matthew 5.38 (cf. Luke 6.29), Exodus 21.24. On what follows, see my *The New Testament and Rabbinic Judaism*, pp. 254ff., *Civil Disobedience in Antiquity*, 1972, pp. 109f., and *Ancient Jewish Law*, 1981, pp. 86ff.

2. See e.g. W. F. Albright and C. S. Mann, *Matthew* (Anchor Bible), 1971, p. 68. Belonging to a breed of New Testament students who have no desire to run down Judaism, they are distinctly uncomfortable and add a plea that came up around the turn of the century: retaliation acted as a check on blood feud. But, at best, it had done so in the distant past.

stance is traceable in the pertinent sources. Nor need we rely on external evidence alone: the Sermon itself militates against the facile handling. For one thing, it is not into law reform; its aim is to direct its listeners away from literal ordinance towards ethical and spiritual understanding. For another, suppose the intention were to abolish a regime under which a thug guilty of mutilation has his eye gouged out, his leg cut off or the like: to summarize the new way of doing things by meekness when slapped would be utterly incongruous. The subsequent counsels—if someone sues you for your shirt or bids you accompany him for one mile, let him have your coat as well or go with him two miles, give and lend whenever asked—would be even remoter. No doubt they may be later elaborations. If so, at least the interpolator knows of no connection with talion.

A solid explanation must recognize that, by the time of the Sermon, he who hurt a person was liable to monetary damages, more precisely, five kinds, not, of course, all of them operative in each case: for permanent impairment, for temporary incapacity, for healing expenses, for pain and for shaming. Pain and shaming were relative newcomers in this array, not really—i.e. by our lights—the subject of any Scriptural provision. Indeed, very likely, they came in not long before the New Testament era. Here is how the sages brought pain under the talion formula. The formula ends: 'burning wound for burning wound, crushing wound for crushing wound, bruising wound for bruising wound'.[3] They held that this enumeration of several ways of wounding must add something of consequence to the basic precept of redress—amends for pain, which varies according to the mode in which an injury is inflicted.[4] As for sham-

---

3. The lex Aquilia contemplates *urere, frangere, rumpere.*

4. This line of reasoning is presupposed in Mekhilta on Exodus 21.35, where the duty of reparation is extended to the mere causing of pain, without a wound.

ing—an even more refined item than pain—the final Rabbinic system derives compensation for it in a, to us, phantastic fashion from an injunction in Deuteronomy, decreeing that a woman who, in order to save her husband fighting with another man, takes hold of the latter's genitals, have her hand cut off.[5] There is good reason to assume, however, that originally (and in the popular view perhaps for a long time) it, like pain, was deemed to be covered by the talion edict. Anyhow, as in many ancient laws, so in the Jewish one, it was a slap and suchlike actions that typified a shaming assault. I cannot here go into why the slap comes to be so widely adopted as a standard example, except to note that one factor is precisely the absence of bodily harm outlasting the moment. If you cut off your enemy's ear or nose, however enormous the indignity resulting, it is to some extent overshadowed by the crude, corporeal atrocity. The offensive thing about a slap is just the indignity— hence when a law gets around to enforcing compensation on this ground, it is a most suitable illustration.[6] The Mishnah, under the head of shaming, lays down: 'If a man slapped his fellow, he gives him 200 *zuz*; if with the back of his hand, 400 *zuz*'.[7]

The Sermon takes off from this development of the maxim. Within the new community, if an evildoer humiliates you, far from insisting on the exact amends due to you, you should be ready to suffer yet again. As soon, then, as we take account of how the Old Testament quotation would strike a Jewish audience of the first century A.D., instead of clinging to a stage that had lost all relevance, there is nothing absurd in meekness when slapped as its contrast.

5. Midrash Tannaim on Deuteronomy 25.11, Mishnah Baba Qamma 8.1.

6. This, au fond, is but another facet of the phenomenon I describe in *Studi in onore di Siro Solazzi*, 1948, pp. 139ff.

7. Mishnah Baba Qamma 8.6.

'Eye for eye' etc. had been the breeder of an ever more ex-
tensive claim in the case of a hurt, with, in the end, redress
even for a cuff; it was to this that 'turn the other cheek' opposed an alternative route to go. What is more, the following admonition—if sued for your shirt, give up your coat
as well—fits, is a natural expansion. I am not at all sure it is
the work of a second hand. Should it be, it still remains
comforting that the by far earliest annotator of 'whoever
shall smite you' etc. manifestly takes it as I do.

(Readers under the spell of our modern legal system may
find it difficult to understand how damages for battery
could be disapproved of as an excessive standing on one's
rights. As just explained, however, this application of 'an
eye for an eye' etc. was a novelty in Jewish law at that time.
Whatever its merits, it was bound to interfere with old-
accustomed social ease. As a somewhat comparable action
looming on the horizon today we might think of, say, that
of a ten-year-old child against a parent who has boxed his
or her ears; or, to stray a little afield, that of a child aged
twenty against a parent who chose an inferior school for
him or her or against one whose race or economic condition was from the outset likely to restrict the choice.)

There is a riddle, happily not affecting my main presentation. The Sermon throughout implies that, if only you
explore the Sinaitic commandments in depth, advancing
from letter to spirit, they will turn out already to contain
the new ideals *in nuce*. For example, 'you shall not murder',
if only we take it in fully, already condemns anger. But
how could it possibly be maintained that 'eye for eye' and
so on inculcates meekness? (This problem, *nota bene*, would
be even harder if the quotation were still related to actual
talion.) One conceivable answer is that, as the Exodus provision runs 'you shall give eye for eye' etc., adepts in Rabbinic exposition, when it came to a slap in the face, were
able to treat the victim as the addressee: you, the one who

has been slapped, shall give cheek for cheek. They might invoke in support such snatches from the prophets as 'I gave my back to the smiters and my cheeks to them that plucked off my hair; I hid not my face from affronts and spitting', or 'He gives his cheek to him that smites him, he is sated with indignity'.[8] Too bold a construction? Not bolder than some of those in behalf of resurrection or, if it be objected that less freedom was allowed in interpreting legal texts (*halakhah*) than historical and doctrinal ones (*haggadhah*), not bolder than the recycling of the statute, just mentioned, concerning an interfering wife. Alas, I see no way of getting beyond speculation.

V.   Glutton and Winebibber

So far I have attempted to persuade you that ignorance of what Jewish exegetes made of their material may blunt our insight into the New Testament quotations from it. I now go on to cases where it has resulted in downright failure to recognize the presence of a quotation.

All three Synoptics record strictures on Jesus for his unworthy meal company and on his disciples for not fasting like those of the Baptist and other Pharisees.[1] In a section confined to Matthew and Luke—Q, for short—Jesus chides the people for having equally scorned John who did not eat and drink and him who did; of John they said he had a malign spirit (presumably, of melancholy[2]) and of him that he was 'a man who is a glutton and a winebibber, a friend of

8. Isaiah 50.6, Lamentations 3.30.

1. Matthew 9.10ff., Mark 2.15ff., Luke 5.29ff., 7.36ff., 15.1ff. On the varying addressees of the strictures, see my article in *New Testament Studies* 19 (1972): 1ff.

2. Palestinian Gittin 48c.

publicans and sinners'.[3] It is this strange combination of apparently separate charges which is here of interest.

Let us observe, to begin with, that in its primary thrust at least, the criticism can hardly have been directed against his deviating from John: the latter is never represented as hostile to publicans and sinners. Next, as for the first charge, in two respects it goes substantially beyond that of lack of penance among Jesus's followers adverted to above. For one thing, it is levelled not against them but against himself. For another, to be a glutton and winebibber is far worse, on an entirely different level, than not to fast or, for that matter, than to eat and drink, the phrasing employed in this pericope. Gluttony and winebibbing are vices.

Now while the Book of Proverbs and Sirach impress on us their ruinous nature, Deuteronomy actually gives them a niche in the criminal process: the capital indictment of a depraved son by his parents culminates in 'he is a feaster and a drunkard'.[4] That Jesus's enemies are not just resorting to a ready-to-hand term of abuse but are citing this law be-

---

3. Matthew 11.19, Luke 7.34.

4. Deuteronomy 21.20, Proverbs 23.20f., Sirach 9.9, 18.33. The Gospels put *phagos kai oinopotes*. The LXX in Deuteronomy 21.20 puts *symbolokopon oinophlygei*, and in Proverbs 23.20 *ekteinesthai symbolais* for 'to be a feaster', *esthai oinopotes* for 'to be a drunkard'. In Proverbs 23.21 the Hebrew 'feaster' becomes a *pornokopos*, 'a fornicator', while 'the drunkard' is retained as *methysos*. Greek Sirach 9.9 warns against *symbolokopein en oinoi*, 'feasting at wine' with another man's wife, 18.33 against being a *symbolokopon ek daneismou*, 'a feaster upon borrowing'. Philo, *On Drunkenness* 4.14.359, faithfully quotes the LXX for Deuteronomy 21.20 (following it up with the noun *oinophlygia* in *On the Change of Names* 37.206.609). Mostly, he uses the root *methys* for 'drunkenness'. But there is variety, e.g. *polyoinia* in 6.22.360. 'Feasting', too, is represented by diverse expressions; in this paragraph we find *aplestia gastros*, 'insatiability of the belly'.

comes plain if we consider its then accepted exposition—to the effect that the clause designates, not a mere reveller, but a reveller surrounding himself with godless associates. For Philo, the worst about such a person is that 'he is not only out to do wrong but to join with others in doing wrong'.[5] By around A.D. 300, Abbahu goes as far as to declare that not unless he consorts exclusively with dissolute fellows does the legislator's severity apply.[6] It is in view of this line of interpretation that 'a glutton and a winebibber' is supplemented by 'a friend of publicans and sinners'.

The features noted above now fall into place. The focus is not on the contrast with John. The target of the attack is Jesus and not his disciples. He is not rebuked for neglect of self-mortification nor, indeed, for excessive indulgence in the literal sense: it is difficult to imagine that anyone could ever have thought of this. He is characterized as the stubborn and rebellious son of the code whose crime consists in a general, calculated, incorrigible defiance of those in authority, the feasting and drinking being only its most visible mark. It has been argued that Talmudic jurisprudence defines this son much as psychiatrists since Philippe Pinel define the sociopath, morally deranged though not insane in a way that exempts from culpability.[7] If this is correct—and I think it is—it furnishes strong support to my proposition. The saying as a whole turns out very pointed: John was rejected as giving in to a devil of melancholy, Jesus, the son out of control, as giving in to a devil of disorder.

What conclusions, if any, are to be drawn from this as to the provenance of the invective is beyond the scope of my topic. I will, however, draw attention to a peculiar notice

5. Philo, *On Drunkenness* 7.25.361.
6. Babylonian Sanhedrin 70b.
7. See M. Rotenberg and B. L. Diamond, *Journal of the History of Behavioral Sciences* 7 (1971): 29ff.

which may be relevant to further enquiry. The general insult that he is possessed, that he is with Beelzebub or the like, occurs in all four Gospels. But only Mark briefly introduces his family coming to seize him, on the ground that he is beside himself.[8] This does sound like parents taking the first steps against a rabid son: according to Deuteronomy, before proceeding to a public trial, they must seek to put things right by chastening him—and Philo expressly lists physical restraint as appropriate at this stage.[9]

VI.   For Their Generation

Luke tells us of a tycoon's agent who, about to be dismissed, forgives all debtors a portion of what they owe;[1] and the laudatory treatment he receives for this is justified by the argument that 'the children of this age are wiser than the children of the light for their generation'. The dictum has given enormous difficulty. It disappears as soon as we

8. Mark 3.21. Klostermann, *Markusevangelium*, 36f., rightly regards *existemi* here as a medical term for sick excitement—'ecstasy'. He adds that, as is well known, it can also denote genuine religious enthusiasm. Maybe this range rendered it particularly attractive to the author of the notice: some kind of double meaning. On a probably second-century Hebrew translation of *exo einai* or *exo gignesthai* in the positive sense, see my note in *Niv Hamidrashia*, 1972, pp. 60ff.

9. Philo, *The Special Laws* 2.41.232. On some connection between the Deuteronomic law and the story of Eli's misbegotten sons in I Samuel 1.12ff., see my *Sons and Strangers,* 1984, pp. 13ff.

1. Luke 16.1ff. In what follows, I draw heavily on my essay 'Neglected Nuances of Exposition in Luke-Acts', in *Aufstieg und Niedergang der römischen Welt*, ed. H. Temporini and W. Haase, 1985, pt. II, Principat, vol. 25.3, Religion, pp. 2329ff.

realize that 'for their generation' echoes Noah's description as 'just and perfect in his generation'[2]—taking it the way it was taken by first-century A.D. Jews.

There went on then a struggle between purists and realists, one of their disagreements relating to behaviour externally meritorious but tied up with questionable concerns: the purists deemed it worthless, the realists—within limits—a second-best.[3] Three Lucan parables contain traces of this problem.[4] The Helper at Midnight satisfies his insistent petitioner not from friendship—this is stated in so many words—but because he cannot bear the undignified scene. The Unjust Steward comes to the debtors' help not from compassion but in order to be saved by them from a degrading life. The Unjust Judge takes up the clamorous widow's case though—as is made crystal clear—still caring about neither God nor man, afraid of public humiliation. Basically, in all three cases, the proper conduct is inspired not by moral virtue but by fear of disgrace. Elsewhere I have connected the prominence of this particular motive with the Third Gospel's shame-cultural affiliation.[5] We are in touch here, I suggest, with Wisdom circles of the time between Jesus and the evangelist. For the purpose in hand it is enough to remark that the verdict is realist. What the Helper, the Steward and the Judge end up doing, while definitely flawed, is none the less an outcome deserving commendation.

2. Genesis 6.9.

3. Philo, in his discussion of historical relativity to which I shall return presently, does speak of 'a second prize in the contest'.

4. Luke 11.5ff., 16.1ff., 18.1ff.

5. See my 'Shame Culture in Luke', in *Paul and Paulinism, Essays in Honour of C. K. Barrett*, ed. M. D. Hooker and S. G. Wilson, 1982, pp. 360f.

However, in addition to the conundrum of the right action with an ulterior aim, the two schools debated that of
the person who, living in a degenerate period of history, is
unable, despite endeavours in the right direction, to come
up to the desirable standard. The realists considered their
attitude, making allowance for his environment, to be sanc-
tioned by the line about Noah, splendid 'in his generation'—which signified, they maintained, 'by comparison
with his generation': though not the equal of many later
saints, he is given generous credit by Scripture for his relative excellence. It is in precisely this application—found in
both Philo and the Midrash[6]—that the phrase serves to explain the praise extended to the agent; and, quite likely, the
minuscule change[7] of the original 'in his generation' into
'for [sic] their generation' is designed to ensure the proper
understanding—'for' denoting 'measured against', 'if account is taken of'. Those still belonging to the present
aeon, of whom he is one, considering their surroundings,
rank higher when making such an inadequate effort than
the members of the new community.

The substitution of 'wise' for 'just and perfect' reflects
the central values of the circles to whom we owe this expansion of the parable. It is noteworthy that, with all their
additional speculation, they do remain alive to the authentic message: the urgent need, in the endtime crisis that has
arrived, of seizing the only chance of escape. Noah in both
Testaments is the archetype of such salvation,[8] so an appeal
to his precedent would be highly effective.

There is, of course, a reason the problem of historical
relativity, in contradistinction to that of dubiously motivated services, is brought up only in connection with the

6. Philo, *On Abraham* 7.36ff., Genesis Rabba on 6.9.
7. Of which I made nothing in my essay 'Neglected Nuances'.
8. E.g. Q, Matthew 24.37f., Luke 17.26f.

Unjust Steward. This parable alone deals with the transition of one age into another, the hero setting an example of successful coping. The theme of the other two parables is the force of prayer, the responses of the earthly Helper and earthly Judge providing an inkling of how heaven will respond. No occasion here, as in the parable about transition, for pondering the different standards of different epochs.

Here is the New English Bible's version of the saying, as good an illustration as any of the helplessness resulting when no heed is paid to what the Rabbis made of the ancient texts. 'For the worldly are more astute than the otherworldly in dealing with their own kind'. In the first place, this is not what we find in the Greek. In the second place, read as part of the New English Bible's overall presentation of the parable,[9] it makes the principal, who has just given notice to the bailiff for squandering his property, express admiration for a final downright villainy. Incredible and, in addition, completely divorced from primitive Christian concerns.

VII. He That Is Without Sin

When Jesus confounds the would-be executioners of an adulteress, 'He that is sinless among you, let him be the first to cast a stone at her',[1] he is citing the Book of Numbers. In it, a wife her husband suspects of infidelity is subjected to an ordeal which, should she be guilty, will make her rot away in the most gruesome manner. The statute

9. Which, like all presentations since Jerome, is mistaken; see my 'Neglected Nuances'.

1. John 8.7. For details, see my lecture in *Juridical Review* n.s. 23 (1978): 177ff.

closes: 'And the priest shall execute upon her all this law, and the man shall be clear of sin and the woman shall bear her sin'.[2] The Rabbis were troubled by the crass inequality between the sexes in this area. They resorted to the following rendering of the final passage, just defensible in Hebrew on over-rigid grammatical grounds: 'And if the man is clear of sin, then the woman shall bear her sin'.[3] So she is liable to punishment only if her accuser leads a blameless life. In due course, the more sensitive sages concluded that even where the individual husband's morals were unexceptionable, it was unjust to come down hard on an erring woman while the male world as a whole, man as a species, was given to hedonism; and in the sixties A.D., the most eminent of them, Johanan ben Zaccai, abolished the ordeal altogether.[4] Throughout this evolution, the progressives invoked the prophet Hosea for their cause: 'I will not wreak vengeance on your daughters when they commit whoredom or on your daughters-in-law when they commit adultery, for you yourselves make off with whores and sacrifice with harlots'.[5]

Jesus, then, quotes the verse from Numbers in its current interpretation—at the time the subject of much debate, there being a good deal of resistance—and he extends the principle to the treatment of an adulteress caught in the act, with not a shred of doubt as to her crime. It should be observed that Johanan, too, advocated leniency even in fully proven cases. A simile of his thoroughly approves of a king who, having divorced his adulterous wife, is reminded

2. Numbers 5.30f.

3. Siphre on Numbers 5.31. As in their treatment of Deuteronomy 31.16, about resurrection—see above, under II—so here the desired meaning is attained by wangling *collocatio*, division.

4. Mishnah Sotah 9.9.

5. Hosea 4.14.

by her friends of her lowly origins where she could not learn right from wrong, and who thereupon remarries her.[6] The excuse, incidentally, is realistic, in line with the pleading of historical conditions we came across under VI: it pleads what we nowadays call social ones.

To Jesus, on this occasion, a Scriptural basis is indispensable. His opponents, as quite a few variants expressly inform us, are out to trap him. They reckon, of course, that he will not condone a stoning; but how can he set himself against an ordinance of the Torah? A mere appeal to fairness—which his words have commonly been thought to constitute—would not have been enough to defeat the schemers. He does stir their conscience but only because he is armed with a text in which their luminaries find fairness demanded for a similar situation. Essentially, he beats them on their own ground, much as that other time—discussed above, under III—when he is asked about divorce, again with a view to trapping him. The questioners know his attitude and hope he will get into difficulty seeing that the Torah permits this measure. Here also he prevails, adducing chapter and verse—in the then accepted sense—for the teaching that indissoluble union befits the ideal kingdom.

It may be worth pointing out that the method resorted to against Jesus—a question meant to embarrass you whichever way you answer it—is extremely old both in popular application and in rhetorical art.[7] Jesus himself uses it in the controversy about his authority, when he counter-asks whether the Baptist's activity was from heaven or men. His foes, of course, deem it from men, but if they say so, they will incur the wrath of the populace. Unlike Jesus, they find no way out: 'we cannot tell'.[8]

6. Deuteronomy Rabba on 10.1.
7. Aristotle, *Art of Rhetoric* 2.23.16.1399a, *Sophistical Refutations* 2.12.173a, *Ad Herennium* 2.24.38.
8. Matthew 21.23ff., Mark 11.27ff., Luke 20.1ff.

VIII.   They Ate and Were Satisfied and
         Took Up What Was Left Over

According to the Synoptics, the multitude fed by Jesus—if
we discount minor variations—'ate and were satisfied and
took up what was left over . . .'. John expands this but still
reflects the original summation.[1] Commentators rightly
note the influence of Elisha's feeding of a hundred men who
'ate and left over'.[2] However, this ending contains only two
members—eating and leaving over—in contrast to three
in the Gospels—eating, being satisfied and leaving over.
There is a second Old Testament text in the background:
when Boaz first meets Ruth in the field, at mealtime he
hands her corn and 'she ate and was satisfied and left over'.[3]

  This source has gone unremarked because, to appreciate
its relevance, we have to be aware of what was seen in it by
the Rabbis. A typical interpretation which seems to be
quite early runs: 'She ate, in this world; and was satisfied,
for the days of the Messiah; and left over, for the Age to

  1. Matthew 14.20, 15.37, Mark 6.42f., 8.8, Luke 9.17, John
6.11ff. See my *New Testament and Rabbinic Judaism*, pp. 36ff.
  2. II Kings 4.42.
  3. Ruth 2.14. The LXX here puts its habitual rendering of
śabhaᶜ, 'to be satisfied': *pimplemi*. Occasionally, however, we do
find *chortazo*, e.g. Psalms 17.15 (in LXX 16.15). The latter, incidentally, no doubt represents *śabhaᶜ* also in Tobit 12.9—where a
revised version prefers *pimplemi*. (This version is published by
O. F. Fritzsche, *Kurzgefasstes exegetisches Handbuch zu den Apo-
kryphen des Alten Testamentes, Zweite Lieferung*, 1853, pp. 71ff.)
Matthew, Mark and Luke all offer *chortazo* while John uses
pimplemi. In Matthew 14.20, 15.37, Mark 6.43, the root *pleres* is
met in connection with the baskets 'heaped' with the remains.
John 6.13 employs *gemizo*. This much less frequent verb occurs
twice in 2.7, which reinforces my suggestion (*New Testament and
Rabbinic Judaism*, p. 45) as to a profoundly thought-out approxi-

Come'.[4] In some expositions, Boaz stands for God and
Ruth for her descendant David or the Messiah himself.
Again, the word for 'corn', *qali*, is equated with *qalil*,
which means 'slight'. So Boaz gives her a slight portion
only but miraculously it suffices for her 'to eat, be satisfied
and leave over'.[5] For the Jews of the first century, then, the
two feedings by Elisha and Boaz belonged closely together,
were largely interchangeable, supplemented one another:
they both exhibited the same deeply significant kind of
wonder wrought by God through and for his elect at various stages of salvation. We must not indeed forget that, to
minds untouched by higher criticism, a testimony from
the Book of Ruth, far older than one centering on Elisha,
would appear particularly venerable and reassuring.

It is a rich tapestry the evangelists have woven: to the extent that the passage from Ruth plays a role in their narrative, Boaz, the widow's redeemer, becomes Jesus and
Ruth he redeems becomes the Messianic community.

IX.   The Handmaid of the Lord

Lastly, the annunciation: 'And the angel said . . . The
Power of the Highest shall overshadow you . . . and Mary
said, Behold the handmaid of the Lord'.[1] This exchange assumes yet further depth when we perceive its evocation of
Ruth, the Messiah's ancestress. She pays a nocturnal visit to

---

mation by John of the bread in the episode under notice and the
wine at Cana.

4. Babylonian Shabbath 113b.

5. Ruth Rabba on 2.14.

1. Luke 1.35ff. See my *New Testament and Rabbinic Judaism*,
pp. 26ff.

Boaz, to whom she is not yet married, offering to become his wife: 'I am Ruth your handmaid, spread therefore your skirt over your handmaid, for you are a redeemer'.[2] In Hebrew and Aramaic, the mysterious verb is closely related to 'to overshadow'. They then spend a symbolical wedding night together, without consummation. What it all means in the ancient saga, I have set out elsewhere.[3] For the present discussion, two links with the Lucan chapter are of importance. One, Ruth, in the offer just quoted, is displaying unbounded faith in Boaz: far from taking advantage of her, he will bring about redemption, guide her to her ultimate, exalted fortune. As Naomi put it when she advised the visit: 'He will tell you what you shall do'.[4] The other, while Goethe, romantically and arrogantly thinking of those primitives as children, admired their doings as idyllic, the Jewish sages, more squeamish yet equally unhistorical in their way, were disturbed by an at-first-sight grave breach of modesty on Ruth's part.[5] By dint of their interpretative art, they proved to their satisfaction not only that she committed no such infraction but, indeed, that she was the purest of all women; and, significantly, the phrasing used by her plays a major part in their deliberations. 'I am Ruth your handmaid, spread therefore your skirt over [overshadow] your handmaid' is contrasted, as expressive of the most sublime chastity, with the shameless invitation the wife of Potiphar extends to Joseph: 'Lie with me'.[6] By choosing Ruth's words for the climax of his recital, the New Testament author depicts her as prefiguring Mary.

2. Ruth 3.9.
3. See my *Ancient Jewish Law*, pp. 33ff.
4. Ruth 3.4.
5. Not denying that each has a point; neither claiming that children are necessarily idyls.
6. Genesis Rabba on 39.7.

Let me in conclusion touch on an aspect not directly falling under my topic and yet neither quite without relevance.
It has to do with style which here, however, more clearly
than in many other instances, has been moulded by profound beliefs and feelings. I am referring to the Gospel's
masterly, beautiful delicacy of presentation. We may assume
that the miraculous birth from the first moment provoked
nasty and mocking comments on the part of unbelievers;
and that the introduction of Ruth, recognized as above reproach though with appearances equally against her, was in
large part calculated to rebut them. Yet there is not a single
mention of those low aspersions. It is not as if their existence were denied: that would defeat the purpose. They are
relegated into the background, implied instead of spelled
out, guardedly alluded to by the in themselves lofty terms
'to overshadow' and 'handmaid'. Thus the readers—or, to
be precise, those of them familiar with the heroes and hero-
ines of tradition—would grasp the contention without
being confronted by crude ugliness. Matthew, it should be
noted, is not so reticent: he relates that Joseph, before being
enlightened by a vision, intended to divorce Mary.[7] In Luke,
the angelic mood of the annunciation scene is never broken;
nothing openly mars the picture; the focus is throughout
on the positive, the Spirit's descent and the Virgin's perfect
submission in trust. So successfully is this achieved that, in
the roughly eighteen centuries of the legend's circulation
in a gentile world, the polemical point has stayed totally
submerged.

This mode of shaping the material has a long history.
Two pieces from Genesis and Second Samuel come to
mind. Jacob serves seven years for Rachel. But then, after
the wedding feast, at night, her father substitutes her elder
and less comely sister Leah and it is to her that the bride-

7. Matthew 1.18ff.

groom finds himself joined in the morning.[8] Not a word is said about her participation in the fraud. Obviously, the most docile daughter could not execute that assignment without a considerable contribution of her own. Once more, the troublesome facts are not negated: it would be difficult to do so. They are pushed out of sight. Certainly, we do come across some acute Rabbinic observations[9] and, of course, modern, psychology-oriented reworkers of the story have a ball. None the less, on the whole, the Biblical author manages to deflect our interest, she remains apart, untouched, we just do not think of her—or, for that matter, Rachel's—active involvement. The feat becomes all the more remarkable when we compare the accounts of Sarah's induction into the harems of the kings of Egypt and Gerar.[10] Here it is fully brought out that she cooperates with Abraham in concealing her married status.

Again, David commits adultery with Bathsheba while her husband Uriah is at the front.[11] Pregnancy results, so the king summons him home to bring news of the campaign and, having received his report, suggests he visit his wife before returning to the army. The child would then have appeared to be Uriah's. The latter, however, refuses to indulge in pleasure at a time his comrades are in the field. Whereupon David sends him back, with a sealed letter to the general requesting that Uriah be so placed in battle as to be sure to fall. The text contains no hint at Bathsheba's complicity in the duping scheme. Indeed, somehow, with supreme skill, our mind is kept off that datum. It is by no means denied—it simply does not occur to us. The odious

---

8. Genesis 29.21ff.   9. Genesis Rabba on 29.22.
10. Genesis 12.11ff., 20.2ff.
11. II Samuel 11. See my article in *Novum Testamentum* 24 (1982): 275ff.

reality is that the king could not possibly have encouraged her husband to spend a night with her without first initiating her and being assured of her utmost support.

No doubt there are all sorts of differences between these episodes. To name only one, Mary is innocent, Leah and Bathsheba are guilty. But this does not affect what I am talking about: the veiling of anything base. In the case of Leah and Bathsheba, our attention is directed away from their doings, in that of Mary, even from a suspicion: essentially, the same concern—to protect the holy. It is hardly accidental that the three most striking Scriptural examples have regard to sexual relations and, furthermore, show women as recipients of the reverential treatment. It is in the realm of sex that solicitude about the look of things, shame, originates in hoary antiquity;[12] and at a certain stage of civilisation, definitely reached in the Near East by the second millennium B.C., it is women—those you care for at least—who may be endowed with a sanctity so special as to require dissociation from impurity not only in life but also in speech and writing. As for the Third Gospel in particular, I have already—under VI—cited my thesis[13] that it is far more imbued with refined shame culture than the other Synoptics. The way Mary is defended is typical of this component.

I agree with the avant-garde among the young generation that a cover-up remains a cover-up however nobly motivated. Also that, on closer scrutiny, the motives leading to women being placed on a pedestal turn out to include distinctly ignoble elements. Unless we heed these insights, often neglected, we are apt to caricature the past and

12. See my papers in *Orita* 3 (1969): 33, 40, and 'Shame Culture in Luke', p. 363.
13. In 'Shame Culture in Luke', pp. 355ff.

bungle more than we have a right to in the present. Still, a number of extremists seem to go too far. For one thing, they fail to allow for the individual circumstances of each epoch, its needs, its means, its inevitable limitations. Our own—not excepting our radicals who, paradoxically, remind me a little of the Rabbinic purists[14]—had better hope for this kind of understanding from future critics. For another thing, too much faith is put in simplistic new formulas: to let it all hang out and complete, unselfish equality of male and female. There is no vision that does not conflict with another, there is nothing entirely good or entirely evil, we must weigh and choose at every step. To me, those ancient, basically truthful records of the interaction between the human—frequently, all-too-human—and the divine are a continuous source of inspiration.

Two ironies. First, a pattern similar to that outlined dominates a far from sacred genre: the detective novel which, from beginning to end, is strewn with heavily disguised occurrences. True, the object is not to prevent an image being stained but to test the reader's intelligence: can he spot the clues? In the end, they will all be brought into the open. As one would expect, the fundamental discrepancy in purpose influences not a few details of the technique;[15] but I shall not enlarge.

Second, what demon moves me, who so treasures the devout considerateness of these tales, to undo it by ruthless analysis?

14. See above, under VI.
15. On rereading this paragraph, I notice that I have slipped from style, with regard to Biblical writers, to technique when coming to the *Krimi*.

Temple Tax

Matthew's four verses about this subject[1] do not rate high in the prevalent opinion, chiefly because the introduction of the fish is uncomprehended—to say the least.[2] A further reason is the neglect of a controversy within Jewry certainly very intense in the thirties but going on right until A.D. 70. The following pages are intended to show that the little section forms a well-constructed whole; that it is definitely part of *Ur*-Christian lore and, indeed, most probably harks

Written for the *Festschrift* in honour of William R. Farmer, to be edited by Ed P. Sanders. I am deeply grateful to William David Davies for criticizing the first draft of this paper. Whether he is less skeptical about the present one I dare not guess.

1. Matthew 17.24ff. See my 'Responsibilities of Master and Disciples in the Gospels', *New Testament Studies* 19 (1972): 13ff., and 'Fraud No. 3', in *The Legal Mind, Essays for Tony Honoré*, ed. N. MacCormick and P. Birks, 1986, p. 15.

2. It might be worth while, as a contribution to *Wissenschaftsgeschichte*, to study the diverse methods (including silence) of dealing with this embarrassment. Even authors who, as far as the rest is concerned, come close to the approach of this paper—e.g. G. A. Buttrick, 'The Gospel According to St. Matthew, Exposition', in *The Interpreter's Bible*, vol. 7, 1951, pp. 465f., and Eduard Schweizer, *Das Evangelium nach Matthäus*, 1976, pp. 231ff.—are at a loss when it comes to the haul.

back to an actual occurrence; and that the fish makes perfect sense in a directive of eminent practical and spiritual importance for the earliest believers.

The collectors of the Temple tax accost Peter. What they say is translatable in two ways between which it is fortunately not necessary to decide: 'Your teacher does not pay the half-shekel' or 'Does your teacher not pay the half-shekel?'. If we go by the first alternative, they assume resistance; but even the second presupposes suspicion—they would not be surprised by Jesus opting out, they are on the attack. The challenging of a disciple for his master's aberrations is a universal phenomenon. A Jungian is expected to defend Jung's response to the Third Reich, a devotee of Est Werner Erhard's socialising. In the first two Gospels Jesus's disciples are interrogated why he eats with publicans and sinners.[3] Peter's 'Yes', however, quickly stops the confrontation. No doubt he thinks that Jesus cannot be remiss, though he may be far from sure about the ins and outs. It is likely, moreover, that his desire to get rid of the officers without ado plays a part in the terse affirmation.

As he returns from the encounter, ere he can report, Jesus divines his perplexity and enlightens him. At first sight, one might infer that we have to do with the type of disciple who does not dare or know to ask and whose interest is to be aroused by the teacher. This type figures in the ancient Seder, from where it is taken over into Mark's day of questions: 'And no one dared any longer ask him, and Jesus, commencing the discourse, said'.[4] Yet the set-up be-

3. Matthew 9.10ff., Mark 2.15ff., restructured in Luke 5.29ff. See my 'Responsibilities of Master and Disciples', pp. 11ff.

4. Mark 12.34f. See my *The New Testament and Rabbinic Judaism* (1956; rept. 1973, pp. 148ff.; 'The Earliest Structure of the Gospels', *New Testament Studies* 5 (1959): 180ff.; *He That Cometh*, 1966, pp. 8ff.; and 'Zukunftsmusik', *Bulletin of The John Rylands University Library of Manchester* 68 (1985): 58ff.

fore us is not quite the same. For one thing, whereas both
in the Seder and in the Marcan analogue, the problem does
not enter the disciple's mind till his attention is called to it,
in the Temple tax story, he comes upon it himself. Again,
whereas both in the Seder and in the Marcan analogue, the
master refrains from unravelling the knot—his task being
to get the disciple to cogitate—in the Temple tax story,
Jesus does so. Lastly, maybe Peter would have asked, only
that Jesus 'anticipates him', gets in first. This action, as we
shall see, is indeed of no mean import. It sets the tone: he
has rare powers at his command. We may compare his spon-
taneous taking up of the dispute among his disciples as to
which of them will be the greatest in the kingdom—found
in Mark and Luke;[5] also, though it is less close, his precise
acquaintance with the home life of the Samaritan woman
in John.[6]

The handling of the Temple tax, he explains to Peter, is a
far from simple matter and the 'Yes' stands in need of a vital
qualification. He begins his instruction by setting out the
latter: ideally, he and his are not bound at all. He reasons
that earthly kings exact tribute from strangers only and not
from their sons. By analogy, as he and his are sons—scil.
of the heavenly King, the Temple's sovereign—they must
be free.

The antithesis between son or member of a family and
stranger is common both in Greek and in Hebrew. Hero-

5. Mark 9.33f., Luke 9.46ff. Not in Matthew 18.1ff.: the dis-
play of extraordinary perception in the Temple tax piece suffices.
It has long been seen that there is a genetic tie between 'And when
they were come to Capernaum . . . and when he [Peter] was come
into the house' in Matthew 17.24f. and 'And he came to Capernaum and being in the house he said to them' in Mark 9.33.
(None of it in Luke.) Which of the two descends from which may
here be left open.

6. John 4.17ff.

dotus[7] tells of a woman whose entire kinsfolk are under sentence of death. Darius, moved by her continual laments (one is reminded of the Lucan judge[8]), allows her to pick one of the lot to live. She names a brother, whereupon he enquires why she chooses one who is 'more a stranger than your children'. Hosea speaks of bastards as 'sons that are strangers',[9] and the stricken Job is accounted 'a stranger' by his own household.[10] Particularly relevant, however, is the attachment in Jewish religion of the label stranger to a non-priest, frequent from Exodus, 'a stranger shall not eat thereof',[11] through Sirach, 'but strangers [Korah, Dathan and Abiram] were incensed against him [Aaron]',[12] to the Talmud where, indeed, we find a derivative added, an abstract, strangeness, signifying the quality of being a non-priest.[13] Such a formation testifies to considerable reflection and discussion upon the area. The point here is that, in Jesus's time, the priests insisted on exemption from the Temple tax,[14] doubtless as 'belonging' in a fashion incompatible with this obligation on strangers. The reverberations of this issue in fragmentary reports and allusions— several of which will be inspected—give us an idea of just how hotly and widely it was debated. To some degree, it appears, he is casting himself and his followers in a similar role.

Several other groups were immune: women, slaves, minors, gentiles and Samaritans. In all five cases, we have to do with a *privilegium odiosum*, a benefit that is really a degrada-

---

7. Herodotus, *Histories* 3.119.   8. Luke 18.1ff.

9. Hosea 5.7.   10. Job 19.15, 17.

11. Exodus 29.33.   12. Sirach 45.18.

13. E.g. Babylonian Yebamoth 68b towards the beginning.

14. Mishnah Sheqalim 1.3f. See H. L. Strack and P. Billerbeck, *Kommentar zum Neuen Testament aus Talmud und Midrasch*, 4 vols., 1924–1929, rept. 1969, 1:762f. *Hophshi* and *eleutheros* denote similar freedom already in I Samuel 17.25.

tion.[15] A specimen from our day is the non-conscription of asthmatics and homosexuals. There was, moreover, within the five a division into two ranks. Women, slaves and minors, though under no duty, yet might make payment of their own will; whereas none was accepted from gentiles and Samaritans—they were right outside, with no stake in the community. (No need here to go into fluctuations with respect to Samaritans.) To this, too, there are modern parallels. An asthmatic, not too sick, if offering to serve, will not necessarily be rejected; but the army has no room for a homosexual. The priests' contention was on a radically different level from any of these categories: for a privilege in the proper sense, a mark of excellence. They regarded themselves as intimates of the Revered one at whose feet the levy was laid. They were almost recipients of it, standing apart from, above, all the rest, whether payers or nonpayers. So essentially tied to their calling, in their eyes, was the exercise of this distinction that they—or at least the extremists among them—declared unenforced payment by a priest to be a sin, an abdication of their special relationship. Persons dispensed from the draft because of their absolutely vital work in thermonuclear development would be something of a present-age counterpart. Or better, in 1914, the young man at Oxford who, unlike most of his contemporaries, did not volunteer. When a patriotic lady, passing him in the street, reproved him, 'What are you doing here? Why are you not with your comrades in the trenches, defending civilisation against the Huns?', he replied: 'Madam, I am civilisation'.

It is against this background that the reaction of the

15. See my 'Enfant Terrible', *Harvard Theological Review* 68 (1975), 371ff., 'Johanan ben Beroqa and Women's Rights', in *Zeitschrift der Savigny-Stiftung*, 99 (1982), Rom. Abt., 27ff., and 'Fraud No. 3', pp. 4ff.

Pharisees becomes understandable. To them, the attitude summarized was one more instance of unwarranted priestly pretensions—smacking of Sadducean exclusivity. At the academy of Jabneh, one Ben Bukri reported a pre-destruction tradition to the effect that a priest paying voluntarily was committing no sin.[16] Johanan ben Zaccai, the academy's head, now as before advocated an even stronger line: it was sinful for a priest to abstain from paying. The Mishnah's legal ruling, which must have prevailed in the final years of the State whenever the Pharisees had the upper hand, agrees with Johanan, i.e. priests ought to pay; none the less 'one does not compel them, for the sake of the ways of peace'.[17] Relaxations in order to avoid ill-feeling are no rarity in Rabbinic—or New Testament—teaching;[18] the very pericope here studied ends up with one, on the part of those who feel unjustly taxed. It is worth noting, however, that, possibly, a variant of the Mishnah's compromise, preserved in the Jerusalemite Talmud, reflects a stage when the priests' aspirations still enjoyed a measure of recognition. Instead of 'the ways of peace', we meet here the far less usual term 'the ways of honour': indicating, possibly, less a mitigation of a principle than a genuine relief on account of exalted vocation.[19] After all, vestiges of their past glory

16. Ben Bukri is known only for this testimony, cited, besides Mishnah Sheqalim 1.4, in Babylonian Menahoth 21b f., 46b, Arakin 4a.

17. Mishnah Sheqalim 1.3f. and, consistent with it, 1.6.

18. See my 'Pauline Contributions to a Pluralistic Culture', in *Jesus and Man's Hope*, ed. D. G. Miller and D. Y. Hadidian, 1971, 2:233ff.

19. Such distinctions as that between interrupting one's prayer to greet somebody from fear and doing the same in acknowledgment of his honour are pertinent: Mishnah Berakoth 2.1 and accompanying Gemara. 'The honour of kings' occurs in Babylonian Berakoth 19a.

survive in fairly late statements—e.g. a fourth-century one, that the priests, when officiating, were representatives, not of the congregation before God, but of God before the congregation.[20]

In debate with Johanan ben Zaccai, prior to the catastrophe, the priests appealed to an injunction in Leviticus[21] according to which offerings brought by them for themselves must be totally burnt, without any portion being eaten. Quite a few offerings, their argument went, as for example the showbread, the ingredients of which the Temple purchases with its revenue,[22] are expressly given over to them as food in the Pentateuch.[23] If they contributed to the revenue, they would be helping purchase these offerings,[24] ergo be bringing them—in part at least—for themselves, ergo be precluded from eating them. Seeing that, on the contrary, they are encouraged to do so, it follows that they must have no hand in the purchase. The conclusion: they may not lawfully participáte in the tax. It would be naive to think that the provision in Leviticus and the tortuous ratiocination taking off from it were the actual root of their claim. The latter came first and was perhaps in existence for centuries before being pegged to the Pentateuch.[25] Roughly, from Hillel on, any regulation, to be fully binding, had to be based on a Scriptural law. Mat-

20. Babylonian Yoma 19a f., Qiddushin 23b, Nedarim 35b. See Strack and Billerbeck, *Kommentar*, 3:4, and 4, pt. 1: 150.

21. Leviticus 6.16.

22. Confirmed by Josephus, *Jewish Antiquities* 3.10.7.255.

23. Leviticus 24.9.

24. It would be interesting to examine this construction within a history of legal personality in Jewish law.

25. The Roman priests who protested against being taxed in 196 B.C.—Livy, *From the Founding of the City* 33.52.4—had no Pentateuch to support them.

tathias, for instance, and his entourage had allowed their troops to fight on a Sabbath if attacked, after experience showed that, otherwise, the Syrians would simply annihilate them; and there is no indication that they invoked a Mosaic ordinance. Some hundred and fifty years later, however, Hillel managed to prove from Deuteronomy that a Jewish army need not interrupt a siege on a Sabbath. This code forbids the use of fruit-bearing trees for siegeworks, adding: 'only those not for food, with them you shall build bulwarks against the city until it be subdued'. 'Until it be subdued': that is to say, according to Hillel, without desisting on a Sabbath.[26] An interpretation manifestly superimposed on, not generated by, the original tenor—just like the priests'. Again, when Jesus's disciples pluck corn on a Sabbath, in all three Synoptics he supports them by referring to David and his band who, as they suffered hunger, ate the showbread reserved for the sanctuary. In Matthew, he appends a justification from what may be read 'in the law'. In the Book of Numbers, the Temple priests are supposed to break the Sabbath, say, for the slaughter of sacrifices. What is now involved, he urges, is greater than the Temple, ergo plainly supersedes those rules. The conclusion: the plucking of the corn is licit. Once more, a highly refined syllogism, employing the technical step *a minori ad maius*, not at all envisaged by the old text.[27] The derivation from the Torah of the prohibition of suicide (subscribed to by Hamlet when he deplores 'the Everlasting's canon 'gainst

26. I Maccabees 2.39ff., Josephus, *Jewish Antiquities* 12.6.2.276f., 13.1.3.12f., Deuteronomy 20.20, Tosephta Erubin 4.7. See my 'Texts and Interpretation in Roman and Jewish Law', *Journal of Jewish Sociology* 3 (1961): 9, 15.

27. Matthew 12.1ff., Mark 2.33ff., Luke 6.1ff., I Samuel 21.1ff., Numbers 28.9f. See my *New Testament and Rabbinic Judaism*, pp. 67ff.

self-slaughter') and the duty of procreation (in the Bible, a blessing) are of the same nature.[28] The number of these cases is large; enormous if we include all the slightly less extreme ones, where the passage resorted to contains some element at least of what is made of it. A systematic exploration would throw much new light on the evolution of the Rabbinic edifice.

The assumption by Jesus and his circle of priestly status of some sort is traceable from early on in so many different strata of the New Testament that—discounting any reinforcement from the Dead Sea Scrolls—its beginnings may safely be ascribed to his lifetime. It is indeed met in his quotation, just adverted to, of the precedent set by David and his retinue who, in an emergency, ate the priests' showbread. The implication is that their overriding task entitled them, even obliged them, to act thus, they were directly engaged in executing God's Messianic plan,[29] and now it is Jesus and his faithful who occupy this place. The additional plea, from precept (the Book of Numbers) instead of from example (David's boldness), puts the notion in more explicit terms: the Sabbath restrictions, suspended for the priests serving in the Temple, must a fortiori not stand in the way of a greater service, greater priests. The 'cleansing'

28. See supra, 'The Old Testament in the New: A Jewish Perspective', pp. 1ff., where the reading back of the ban on suicide into the Ten Commandments is noted, and my *The Duty of Procreation*, 1977, pp. 1ff., 42.

29. It would not be surprising if pious scribes of Jesus's era had taken David's declaration in I Samuel 21.3, 'The king has commanded me a business', in the sense not of 'Saul has commanded me' but of 'God has commanded me'. For one thing, on this basis David would not be guilty of deception. That the interpretation is not preserved may be due precisely to the use made of the episode in the Gospels. But, of course, one cannot build on this speculation.

of the Temple with, in Mark, prominence accorded to a technical detail of the daily priestly business,[30] is another strong piece of evidence.

Jesus is not willing to waive the prerogative: this is the major premise he impresses on Peter. From here, however, he goes on to a formidable complication. A downright refusal of the administration's demand might put off[31] people not otherwise hostile—interfering with his mission. No doubt there are conditions in which a path must be continued regardless. But the Temple tax does not fall under them, hence creates a dilemma. He solves it by devising a course which formally, in semblance, amounts to perfect compliance, so will avoid any discord while, in reality, they part with nothing that is genuinely their own, so are not subjecting themselves to the impost. The latter is to be satisfied with a coin Peter will take from the mouth of the first fish he catches. Whosoever it was in the past, it became ownerless when the fish carried it off, and now it falls to the finder. It can, therefore, be validly employed to discharge a debt and—equally important—no uninitiated will be aware of anything out of the ordinary. Nevertheless, as far as substance is concerned rather than image, no concession is made. Economically and psychologically, the passing on of money coming from nowhere and the group's property for a fleeting moment only, just long enough to fulfil the purpose of appeasing an environment of deficient insight, is not a true contribution on their part.

30. Mark 11.16, a provision singled out by the priest Josephus, *Against Apion* 2.8.106.

31. *Skandalizo*: when it has its full weight, 'to give offence to somebody leading to his alienation, missing the right way, stumbling'; at times, little more than 'to give offence to somebody'— our modern 'to scandalize'. See G. Stählin, art. 'Skandalon, Skandalizo', *Theologisches Wörterbuch zum Neuen Testament*, ed. G. Friedrich and others, vol. 7, 1964, pp. 343ff.

Dodges of this pattern were familiar in that period. Here is one dating from before the middle of the first century B.C. and going on for hundreds of years.[32] Under the austere Roman reglement of insolvency, infamy befell not only an actual bankrupt but also a debtor who got his creditor to be content with a percentage. A creditor wishing to spare his debtor this punishment would cooperate in the following procedure. Say, the debtor owed 1200 and all he had was 200. He paid 200 and the creditor immediately returned it, by way of gift. The debtor then paid it again, to get it back again as a gift. And so on—and only the sixth payment was kept by the creditor. Formally, in semblance, the debtor had now paid in full. But 1000 out of the 1200 were, so to speak, brought along by a fish, provided to him for just the brief hour of the transaction, economically and psychologically not a true disbursement by him. A Talmudic anecdote,[33] where it is not payment that is simulated but acceptance of a gift, is worth quoting here because the reason for staging the make-believe is to forestall the would-be donor's resentment: reminiscent of Jesus's reason for feigning conformity. On a pagan festival, Jews were to refrain from any dealings that might boost the thanksgiving to idols—such as lending or making a present to a pagan. Some Rabbis worried even about receiving a present since even this might make the pagan rejoice and bless his gods. When Judah II (grandson of Judah the Prince) on such a festival was sent a gold piece by a pagan acquaintance, he asked Resh Laqish who happened to be with him: 'If I do accept, he may render thanks to his idol, if I do not, he will conceive enmity against me'. At Resh Laqish's advice, he took the piece but at once, while the messenger was still there, dropped it

32. Digest 46.3.67, Marcellus XIII digestorum. See my *Roman Law*, 1969, pp. 93f., and 'Fraud No. 3', p. 14.
33. Babylonian Aboda Zara 6a, cited by Strack and Billerbeck, *Kommentar*, 1 : 885.

into a well as if by accident. Thus the donor, on being told, could not be insulted—since his gift was accepted—but neither would he be moved to praise his idol—since no sooner was it accepted than lost. It was 'accepted' in inverted commas, for a few seconds, so no animosity would ensue.

Modern commentators tend to overlook the fact that Jesus is supplying an illustration, a model, and that it is offered not for literal imitation but for imitation as to its substantive content, its message—namely, that while the position of this special priesthood is inabdicable, it must be exercised gently. Au fond, it accords with the counsel: 'Be subtle as the serpents and harmless as the doves', which, curiously, like the Temple tax narrative, is preserved only in Matthew.[34] His sending out of Peter for a coin the first fish will present draws on his superior capacity of being informed about odd circumstances, certainly not meant to be reproduced. As noticed above, the session opens by his realizing what has occurred without being told. This is a peculiar knowing of past and present. His mandate regarding the coin actually implies a foreknowing—such as he manifests when he predicts to the disciples preparing his entry into Jerusalem that they will find a colt tied for his use[35] and to those looking for a room for his Passover meal that they will meet a guide.[36] Of course, once he is gone, the community cannot rely on a magical haul. But this does not dispense them from heeding the core of the lesson. They will have to contrive mundane, ever varying ruses enabling them to reconcile the conflicting requirements—to live up to their election at once and not upset the ignorant. It is the

34. Matthew 10.16.
35. Matthew 21.2ff., Mark 11.2ff., Luke 19.30ff.
36. Mark 14.13ff., Luke 22.10ff., considerably reduced in Matthew 26.18f.

master alone who may choose a shortcut bordering on the miraculous for the exemplary precedent. For one thing, in this way, it can be flawless—as even the best-intentioned schemes lacking supernatural assistance seldom are.[37] It should be observed that this mode of instruction is evidenced among the Tannaites. The clearing up of a complex of questions by Gamaliel II, successor of Johanan ben Zaccai as president of Jabneh, involved his astounding identification of a person he had never seen before: 'He recognized him through the holy spirit and from his words we learnt three things'.[38]

In the most fundamental respect, Jesus's attitude to tribute to Caesar is at one with that just outlined. Caesar does occupy an elevated rank, but when his bidding clashes with God's, God must prevail: in the maxim to pay 'what is Caesar's to Caesar and what is God's to God', the emphasis is on the final words. Often, here too, the best course will be to be serpent as well as dove, to get along by means of loopholes.

(Wolfgang Kunkel[39] lived up to it in the Second World War. He was a Military Judge in the East. In 1943 one captain denounced another one for having listened to the Moscow radio a year previously: a capital crime. What prompted him to come forward at that moment was that

37. Take the one mentioned above, where creditor and debtor colluded to save the latter from infamy. The earlier jurists did not pass it: they decided that, as 1000 came in effect from the creditor's funds, it remained a case of insolvency. By contrast, even these diehards would have had no complaint about money furnished to the debtor by a god or, for that matter, discovered inside a fish.

38. Tosephta Pesahim 1.27, Palestinian Aboda Zara 40a, Babylonian Erubin 64b, Leviticus Rabba on 27.2.

39. A sketch of his personality by Dieter Nörr may be found in *Gedächtnisschrift für Wolfgang Kunkel*, ed. D. Nörr and D. Simon, 1984, pp. 9ff.

the culprit had just been appointed *Bahnhofskommandant*, i.e. was given charge of a little railstation. Terrifying: the degree by which this put him ahead of the accuser was minuscule; and so, of course, was either's life expectancy. Kunkel did not want to pronounce sentence of death. The trouble was that his verdict would have to be approved by higher-ups behind the front, and they were ruthless. It would have been no use, for example, to point to the promotion as proof that the man was doing his duty to the full. Yet he found a way. The decree which ordained the death penalty was issued *für den grossdeutschen Raum*, 'for the greater German realm'. The area around Moscow was not part of this, but again, to simply state this and acquit would not have sufficed: the Berlin authorities would have rejected it as formalistic and weak-kneed. Kunkel declared the decree inapplicable because the Moscow area was *noch nicht*, 'not yet', incorporated in the *grossdeutsche Raum*. By phrasing it thus, he appeared to be absolutely confident of the outcome: it was only a matter of a few clean-up operations. To make doubly sure, and no doubt also to teach the informer a lesson, he added a rider in which he severely censured the latter for waiting so long before bringing so serious an offence to the attention of his superiors. The judgment was duly confirmed.)

Indeed, Jesus's reply itself is 'subtle', serpent-like, so framed that while sympathizers will appreciate where priority is placed, no easy pretext for intervention is handed to the government. Significantly, in Mark, this section corresponds to that of the Seder exhibiting the type of disciple concerned about law, and he also receives a cryptic answer.[40] The opacity of the saying is underlined by the contradictory meanings attributed to it already in New Testament

40. Mark 12.13ff. See the writings listed in footnote 4.

times. According to Luke,[41] it was used in Jesus's arraignment before Pilate, distorted into an unambiguous No to Roman taxation. In Romans,[42] it is pretty much the opposite. (Admittedly, juristic acumen can turn around the clearest dictum. A forthright Mishnaic paragraph treats murderers, robbers and excise-gatherers as equally deserving to be misled. The Gemara transmits an exegesis of it which, deferring to Caesar like Romans, virtually annuls the part as to publicans.[43]) Of course, notwithstanding the profound affinity, there are bound to be major dissimilarities between the two cases. One is that, Caesar being a heathen tyrant, whatever may speak against submitting to his tribute, it cannot be his fatherhood; nor can we expect from Jesus a warning against 'putting him off'. Another, that, in the Gospel framework, the question respecting Caesar emanates from hostile outsiders, whereas that respecting the Temple is gone into within the inner circle. As a result, the answer to the former has to remain on a general level, whereas that to the latter follows up the governing principle with specific, practical guidance.

In conclusion, some remarks on setting. Few nowadays deny that the first half of the pericope goes back to before the destruction. After it, the conquerors appropriated the tax, diverting it to heathen worship.[44] To take the argument as envisaging this *Fiscus Judaicus* will not do. No first-century Christian author can have thought of the saved ones

41. Luke 23.2, prepared for by 20.20. See J. M. Creed, *The Gospel According to St. Luke*, 1930, p. 247. The historicity or otherwise of the notice is immaterial in the present connection.

42. Romans 13.6f.

43. Mishnah Nedarim 3.4, Babylonian Nedarim 28a.

44. Josephus, *Jewish War* 7.6.6.218, Suetonius, *Lives of the Caesars*, Domitian 12.2, Dio Cassius, *Roman History* Epit. 65.7.2.

as sons of the Emperor to whom it went, and to be sons of the Highest would be irrelevant if the tax was not his.

The second half is mostly treated as an eccentric appendage. There is a tendency, moreover, to postulate relatively late elements both in it and in the first. If the foregoing exposition is approved, the pre-destruction date holds good for the pericope in toto, including the catch—essential to the complete, down-to-earth teaching. As for the late elements, the arguments are unconvincing. Jesus's repudiation of liability is alleged to evince a disdain for the Temple at variance with his zeal as he 'cleanses' it.[45] In reality, his stand founds on the conviction that he and his are its truest priests. The view here combated would mean (unless the comparison he draws is quite off, *hinkend*) that the sons of earthly kings are left untroubled by the treasury because they despise the throne; whereas, palpably, the reason is their closeness to it, their share in it. It would mean also that, when Jesus, in defence of his disciples, cites the eating of hallowed food by David and his men, he is depicting them as scornful of the sanctuary—not credible. They were, indeed, at this moment its most devoted fighters, precursors of Jesus's group. This is not to exclude the possibility that the preservation (precarious, via Matthew only)

45. See e.g. E. Lohmeyer, *Das Evangelium des Matthäus*, ed. W. Schmauch, 1956, p. 275; F. V. Filson, *A Commentary on the Gospel According to St. Matthew*, 1960, p. 195; Stählin, 'Skandalon, Skandalizo', pp. 350f. Basically similar is the position of C. H. Dodd, *History and the Gospel*, 1938, pp. 90ff.: The story 'of the Coin in the Fish's mouth is pertinent to the question of the payment of the Temple tax by Jewish Christians who no longer felt themselves to be within the Jewish community. That question is hardly likely to have become acute in the stage of Church life represented by the early chapters of Acts, and still less likely during the lifetime of Jesus. The story is suspected, not without good reason, of being a later accretion'.

of the incident owes something to precisely this misinterpretation of it as documenting contempt. Again, the prominence of Pauline ideas is noted as militating against the first half of the century: the Christian's freedom from the law as a child of God and the yielding in order not to cause the weak to stumble.[46] But it may be Paul who is secondary. The freedom theme in the Temple tax story is far less developed than in his writings; and all the three Synoptics carry strong pronouncements by Jesus against putting off the little ones.[47]

W. D. Davies lists the second half among the Matthean revisions by which a Jesuanic absolute is toned down, to make it livable with; it is akin, as he sees it, to Paul's procedure anent tribute to Caesar.[48] The parallel, however, is illusory. Jesus's saying about the tribute guardedly (since ill-wishers are listening) recommends a bending which, however, must never be such as to detract from the principal allegiance; Paul bids us pay.[49] By contrast, Jesus's saying about Temple tax openly (since he is addressing a confidant) denies its bindingness and the practical solution following on it (again, not needing to be veiled) is in line, not with Paul, but with the original, cautious word about the tribute: do make the requisite gesture without, however, any surrender of substance. This latter agreement, already mentioned above, sets the case apart from others where Davies is right. He takes no account of the fish. It may be worth observing that, even if it were due to Matthew, this manner of procuring the tax ought to be credited

46. See e.g. S. E. Johnson, 'St. Matthew, Exegesis', *Interpreter's Bible*, 7:465f.

47. Matthew 18.6, Mark 9.42, Luke 17.2.

48. W. D. Davies, *The Setting of the Sermon on the Mount*, 1964, pp. 389ff.

49. With a powerful underpinning, so there be no breach.

with the goal here postulated: appeasement but no stepping down. It would still be, not some extravaganza, but a standard for an embattled community to emulate. To this extent, that is, the gist of my thesis would remain unaffected.

A number of traits do strongly favour a very early origin of the whole—the nature of the band in particular. As already pointed out, the collectors expect Peter to account for Jesus's conduct. Furthermore, they speak of 'your teacher' with 'your' in the plural: any one of the disciples represents all the others. Nor is this all. In expounding the situation, Jesus does not differentiate between himself and his followers: they are all equally of the family of the Temple's Lord. By the same token, the coin he foresees will be a *stater*, a full shekel, to serve in one go on behalf of both himself and Peter;[50] and doubtless, qua recipient of the

---

50. For B. H. Streeter, *The Four Gospels*, new ed., 1930, p. 504, the *stater* supports an Antiochene provenance of the pericope: it seems that only at Antioch and Damascus was this coin worth exactly two half-shekels. But, first, the evidence is shaky. Secondly, the *stater* is customarily equated with a full shekel, so at any rate near enough. Third, the half-shekel being seldom coined in Jesus's time, it may indeed have been quite usual for two persons to combine and pay with a *stater*: see A. H. McNeile, *The Gospel According to St. Matthew*, 1955, p. 257. Lastly and above all, even if the *stater* hails from Antioch, by itself it proves nothing for the bulk of the narrative. 'When I worked on fables, I was amused by the transformation of animals in the course of migration. The longbeaked bird that removes a bone from the wolf's throat is a heron in Babrius, a crane in Phaedrus, a stork in La Fontaine. Joshua ben Hananiah speaks of an Egyptian partridge; and the wolf becomes a lion—symbolizing Rome or the Emperor Hadrian. None the less the body of the paradigm stays the same throughout': see my *Ancient Jewish Law*, 1981, p. 22. Valuta is at least equally exchangeable. Streeter himself describes the point as of merely 'infinitesimal' significance.

model advice on how to cope, Peter once more stands for his fellows as well. Such a presentation suggests a time when the group was small and close-knit and before the crucifixion had rendered the master more distant. Perhaps the latter point can be made more concrete by adducing again the Matthean expansion with Jesus's statement[51] that 'here is something greater than the Temple'. From the sixth century on, we meet the reading 'somebody greater'. The Temple tax episode is unmistakably conceived in terms of 'something greater'.

Peter's appearance may have to be taken seriously. If he were singled out just for retrieving a bonus from a fish, that might be brushed aside by reference to his former trade. But he is on stage from the first, when probed by the officials. There is reason to believe that Mark's day of questions derives from a Seder where Peter fitted sayings of Jesus into the pre-established liturgy.[52] The opening topic is tribute to Caesar. Quite possibly, then, Peter heard about the related topic of the Temple tax, too, from Jesus. I Peter, it should be recalled,[53] contains what sounds like an echo of the scene here analysed: the Christians are looked upon as the choice Temple and priesthood and as such, indeed (by now Jesus has been crucified and the battle lines are drawn), a rock putting off[54] unbelievers.

At any rate, two basic considerations seem scarcely disputable. One, the Temple tax problem must have been terribly hard, on every level, for Jesus and those around him. Two, whatever Jesuanic tradition existed concerning it is likely to have crystallized, say, around A.D. 40, in those years, that is, when the community would badly want to hear about what it owed to the foreign regime and the na-

51. Matthew 12.6.
52. See my 'Zukunftsmusik', pp. 61ff.
53. I Peter 2.4ff.   54. *Petra skandalou.*

tive Temple rulers, an unholy alliance between whom had just contrived the death of its head. Even Paul, preaching obedience to the State, still focuses on tax as the ultimate criterion.[55] For one who disagrees with Bill's affirmation of the overall priority of Matthew, it is gratifying to be able to write up for his *Festschrift* an occurrence as authentic as anything in Mark. It is one of very few such instances, left-overs, one imagines, from the Hebrew precursor.

55. Romans 13.1–7.

The Burdened Convert

Paul deems a convert a new creation. What, then, are we to make of his searing self-reproach for what he did to the Christians before joining them? 'I am not meet to be called an apostle because I persecuted the church of God'.[1] It is an anguish that never abates, attested in Acts as well as his own writings.

I

The easy reply that the newness is mainly metaphorical will not do. For the Rabbis of his time, conversion—by circumcision and baptism in the case of males, baptism alone in that of females—was a true, miraculous rebirth, and he is no less serious about it. In his view as in theirs, a convert's entire past is gone: all connections good or bad, rights, duties, sins. A shying away from this extremism, plus unfamiliarity with the Jewish model, have produced odd puzzles and distortions in studies of the Epistles, I Corinthians in particular. As instances of major consequence I

To Eric and Tina.

1. I Corinthians 15.9.

single out (a) the convert and his or her original family, (b) the convert and his or her original marriage.[2]

To begin with, as for the Jewish structure.[3] (a) Nothing links a convert to the original family—obviously, seeing he or she has just come into existence. One result is that if, say, a heathen household convert en bloc, incest prohibitions no longer apply and the closest relations—relations no longer—may intermarry. However, it was found that this freedom gave rise to misunderstandings among the unthinking: they might gain the impression that Judaism took incest lightly. The sages, therefore, ordained that proselytes must abstain from such unions as were illicit in the surrounding culture. This did not, let us note, encroach on the principle. For example, notwithstanding the restriction, a brother and a sister both of whom convert and then marry still become husband and wife—only if they act from defiance, they will be excommunicated, and if from ignorance, he will be bidden to divorce her. (b) The pre-conversion marriage survives as little as the pre-conversion family: the convert is simply a different person from the one that was married. In practice, it is true, the impact is often less trau-

2. See my following writings: *The New Testament and Rabbinic Judaism*, 1956, rept. 1975, p. 113; 'Pauline Contributions to a Pluralistic Culture: Re-Creation and Beyond', in *Jesus and Man's Hope*, ed. D. G. Miller and D. Y. Hadidian, 1971, 2:223ff.; 'Biblical Landmarks in the Struggle for Women's Rights', in *Juridical Review* 90, n.s. 23 (1978): 184ff.; 'Historical Aspects of Informal Marriage', in *Revue Internationale des Droits de l'Antiquité* 25 (1978): 95ff.; *Ancient Jewish Law: Three Inaugural Lectures*, 1981, pp. 14ff.; and 'Onesimos', in *Christians among Jews and Gentiles, Essays in Honor of Krister Stendahl*, ed. G. W. E. Nickelsburg and G. W. MacRae, 1986, pp. 40ff.

3. Principal texts Mishnah Qiddushin 1.1, Niddah 5.4, Palestinian Yebamoth 12a, Babylonian Yebamoth 22a, 48b, 62a, 98b, Sanhedrin 58a ff., Qiddushin 77a ff., Genesis Rabba on 12.2.

matic than might be supposed at first blush. In the New Testament period, the commonest mode of marrying is by intercourse. (It still figures in the Mishnah as number 3, behind money and writ.) Hence if a couple convert both of them and stay together, they are validly married again through that very togetherness. It is indeed 'married again', not 'married still', but mostly the transition will be smooth. I shall not go into exceptional complications.

I Corinthians 5 must be read with (a) in mind. A member of the flock lives with his stepmother, his father's widow. It is plainly done, not in the spirit of moral nihilism then prevalent in some segments of society, but from rapturous delight in the absolutely fresh start: the whole community is 'puffed up',[4] elated, in sympathy with him—a reaction the current commentaries cannot appreciate. Paul condemns it. It goes counter to the cautionary rule to avoid a degree like this, 'in no way among the gentiles',[5] abominated by them—this reference to their standard is also pretty pointless except against the background of the Rabbinic canons. Marvellous as the new creature's opportunities are, Paul insists, he must subordinate them to the welfare of the growing church and not be carried away by self-centered arrogance.

Chapter 7 deals with conversion of one spouse only, and here (b) is relevant. Paul leaves no doubt that the convert is released. Good Rabbinic doctrine: the married person he or she was has ceased to be. At the same time, if the unconverted spouse continues living with the convert, this cohabitation, in Paul's analysis, makes them into a couple again—in accordance with the above-quoted norms as to conclusion of marriage.

Two observations should be added. One, regarding the

4. I Corinthians 5.2.
5. I Corinthians 5.1.

termination of the pre-conversion bond. In the traditional opinion, Paul is thereby infringing Jesus's stand on the indissolubility of marriage. But he is not; it is surely inconceivable that he should be. He adheres to the Rabbinic position, so 'to be a new creation' is more than a trope. The convert is just not identical with the previous incarnation: that is the ground for his or her release. It is much later exegetes who, cut off from their roots and oblivious therefore of the genuine import, substituted divorce. They thus had a deviant teaching on their hands which they defensively titled 'the Pauline Privilege'. My second remark concerns the new marriage if the converted spouse stays on. In this matter, Paul is characteristically and daringly more liberal than the Rabbis. For one thing, he recognizes the union even if the unconverted partner is a heathen. (Adumbrations of this occur in earlier fringe groups.)[6] For another, it is not only a male convert who can 'sanctify',[7] make into a spouse, an unconverted woman, but also a female convert who can 'sanctify' an unconverted man. This directive, I suggest, has a claim to attention whenever Paul's attitude to women is being inspected.

Philemon is another illustration of his sharing the Rabbis' belief in a realistic, supernatural effect of conversion. It has long been noticed that, though not asking Philemon to manumit Onesimos, yet he does ask him to receive him not as a slave but as a brother. The explanation is that a manumission would be superfluous if not offensive. The baptized Onesimos, by virtue of the baptism, is no longer he that was owned by Philemon. The latter, himself guided into the faith by Paul, would understand.

Both Jews and early Christians were denounced by the

6. Testament of Levi 14.6.
7. I Corinthians 7.14.

pagans as practising incest,[8] an accusation historians brush aside as sheer calumny. Unfair. Pagans would derive most of their information about those religions from someone, or the acquaintance of someone, who had gone over and reported back. He or she was bound to dwell on the awesome emergence as another being; and indeed, if belonging to a circle of enthusiasts such as we come across at Corinth, on privileges which, to outsiders, must be indicative of a general, despicable perversion. The sages, we have seen, were alive to the likelihood of misconceptions here. The indictment in question is in fact weighty evidence in support of the picture I am drawing.

As the church became de-Judaized, conversion, once a tornado, changed into a breeze. Above all, it was tamed so as to turn around the inner life only but not life in its totality. While there was still cleansing from fault and granting of spiritual faculties, such worldly things as civic status, relationships, monetary affairs were no longer touched. Probably, even apart from the non-Jewish influence, the development was inevitable when Christianity rose to be the dominant creed. So long as the number of converts was relatively small—as in Jewry and *Ur*-Christianity—a problem like the extinction of inherited blood-ties was manageable. With masses involved, to hold on to the pristine treatment of it would have been too undermining of the established order. A pessimist might class this as yet another case of religion buying security and prosperity by leaving the material, social scene to the powers that be. An optimist will plead that we have to do with one of the prudent concessions—not the same as surrenders—necessary day in, day out, in an imperfect universe.

8. Tacitus, *Histories* 5.5, Athenagoras, *Plea for the Christians* 31.1, Eusebius, *Ecclesiastical History* 5.1.14.

The Jewish law of conversion has undergone no major reform since Pauline days. Suppose, as is by no means impossible, fifty years from now marriage between half-brother and half-sister were legitimized in the Western hemisphere, such a pair of proselytes would be entitled to wed. Still, one cannot help sensing a certain reserve in this field among modern Jewish scholars, as if they were a little ashamed. Hardly surprising: in the climate of rational propriety dominating academia during the two centuries prior to the world wars, to spell out the magical detachment of a convert from the mightiest taboos was to risk feeding into very popular proofs of Talmudic inferiority. Quite likely, it is largely due to this near-silence that the native basis of Paul's design has remained unrecognized till recently. For its Rabbinic material, New Testament research is dependent on Jewish experts, hence apt to break down when these default. Future exploration will no doubt be far less timid, for two curiously disparate reasons: respect for, or at least interest in, thorough renewal from on high is on the increase and, owing to the melting down of the family, the age-old, instinctive horror of incest is lessening.

II

So I come back to Paul's guilt—which, at a cursory glance, almost makes it look as if, in contrast to subsequent generations, he was having more difficulty with the heaven-wrought supersession of the inner man than that of outer conditions. The key to the riddle may lie in a combination of two factors.

First, logic is not everything: it is only natural that, whatever the strict implications of his system, sorrow and, indeed, remorse for fearful evil perpetrated should endure in his heart. Yet this cannot be the whole answer. It might satisfy if these feelings were barely discernible here and there. But they receive the clearest public expression and, moreover, are never relieved by any hint that baptism has made the crooked straight. He is too mindful of his responsibility as instructor to give free rein to wayward sentiments where so momentous a subject is involved. There must be something that renders them appropriate, maybe even the bearers of a lesson for his particular audiences. Secondly, then, he seems to follow a Rabbinic view that what is not wiped out by conversion is the wrong in delaying it once the truth has been taken in.

Josephus reports[9] that the King of Adiabene, though adopting the Jewish faith and devoting himself to the study of Scripture, yet, for a while, with his mentor's approval, did not undergo circumcision—which might provoke a revolt of the populace. What merits attention is that, in principle, to refrain from the act at this stage counts as a dereliction, only because of the extraordinary risks, 'God will grant pardon'. After some time, however, Josephus goes on, another, less accommodating master intervened, charging the king with impiety in reading the Law without following it out. 'How long will you continue to be uncircumcised?' For this rigorist, no excuse is good enough. Both agree on the essential: that he who has clearly heard the summons is henceforth accountable for failing to pay heed.

In the Talmud, the idea is met in a discussion among sages flourishing from towards the end of the first century A.D.[10] They are exercised by the problem that proselytes commonly suffer oppression—hated by those they have left—though, unlike the bulk of the Jews, they do not deserve it, being 'children just born', their past vanished, no blame on their shoulders. One solution is that they lingered

9. *Jewish Antiquities* 20.2.4.38ff.
10. Babylonian Yebamoth 48b.

over the final decision: that stubbornness does enter into
the new state.[11] Nor have we to do here with an extravaganza. Around 300, Abbahu (or his son Hanina) discovers
textual support for this justification of the hardship in store
for proselytes—to wit, in the saga of one who did not lag
and, accordingly, fared well. Ruth, the model convert in
Rabbinic eyes, showed supreme eagerness to be allowed
into the fold; and when Boaz blessed her, 'May your reward be complete, *shelema*',[12] he meant just this—that in her
case the renewal from above would be perfect, unmarred by
hesitation. Abbahu, it may be recalled, often disputes with
Christians.[13]

Possibly, note should be taken of other homilies which
appear to assign a special place to a gentile unerringly pur-
suing conversion. Ruth's appeal to Naomi not to reject her
is interpreted as an appeal 'not to sin over her'.[14] Again, the
Bible has Naomi realize that 'Ruth was steadfastly minded
to go with her'. The phrase 'to go with her', Judah ben Simon holds, indicates that from the moment of her resolve
Ruth was Naomi's equal.[15]

---

11. The verb for 'to linger', *shahah*, has the same range as its
English equivalent, including culpable passivity. Tax evasion by
means of delay occurs in Babylonian Megilla 13b. Numbers
Rabba on 4.19 contains an exegesis of Moses's order to Aaron in
Numbers 17.11: 'Take your fire-pan and carry it quickly unto the
congregation'. Why, the Midrash asks, had it to be done quickly?
Moses saw the angel of death about to strike, hence called out
'Quickly—why do you stand and tarry?'.

12. Ruth 2.12.

13. See W. Bacher, *Die Agada der Palästinensischen Amoräer*,
1896, 2:115ff.

14. Ruth Rabba on 1.16.

15. Ruth Rabba on 1.18. A good illustration of the diverse
uses which can be made of the same idiom. Judah ben Ilai sees in
the notice, Genesis 6.9, that 'Noah went with God' an allusion,

The baptismal catechism preserved in the Talmud recommends that a would-be proselyte be warned not to take the step rashly: it will bring him into a wounded nation and burden him with commandments violation of which entails heavy penalties.[16] Is this inconsistent with the notion of culpable delay? Not necessarily. Frivolous chase after novelty is one thing, genuine insight into a higher world that offers is another. It makes sense to discourage the former, diversion rather than conversion, while considering it a duty to bow to the latter. There is, besides, a fundamental datum: in areas like this, encompassing the mysteries of conscience, choice of path, receptivity to the Lord's bidding, extent of liability, we ought to reckon with an enormous diversity of opinion. Josephus's tale itself supplies an example. The first counsellor admitted a concession (even he, it is true, merely since principled conduct was singularly perilous), the second 'came from Galilee, reputed to be exceedingly strict about the traditions'.

As for Paul, it may be expected that, of all standards feasible, he would prefer the most demanding one—applying it to himself at least if not universally. Nor must we overlook the uniqueness of his experience, adding immeasurably to the gravity of his shortcoming. As he must see his pre-conversion life, he not only kept battling the gospel when fully acquainted with it and its worth but also, in so

---

not to his equality, but to his imperfection: he resembles a toddler dependent on the parent. By contrast, Abraham was told by God, Genesis 17.1, 'Go before me': like an adult (Genesis Rabba on 6.9). See my 'Neglected Nuances of Exposition in Luke-Acts', in *Aufstieg und Niedergang der römischen Welt*, ed. H. Temporini and W. Haase, 1985, pt. II, Principat, vol. 25.3, Religion, p. 2338.

16. See my *New Testament and Rabbinic Judaism*, pp. 113ff., and *Ancient Jewish Law*, pp. 18ff.

doing, spurned 'God's separation of him from his mother's womb'.[17]

Two passages in Acts and a third in I Corinthians concerning blameworthy slowness are reminiscent of the Rabbinic attitude outlined. In Acts 26.14, Jesus addresses him who is still Saul: 'Why do you persecute me? Hard for you to kick against the pricks'. The opening (recorded also in two previous chapters)[18] is a rhetorical question, really an emphatic pointing out of the senselessness of Saul's warfare. *Skleros*, 'hard', and several words containing the root often refer to obduracy; doubtless this meaning plays a part here. Most revealing is the expression 'to kick against the pricks'. Conjuring up an unruly horse's fate, it always denotes the fruitless, self-maiming insubordination of the subject of an all-powerful ruler, man versus God in Pindar and Euripides, citizen versus monarch in Aeschylus.[19] Thus Saul is not approached as a complete outsider yet to be brought into the fellowship. To some degree at least he is indentured already and reminded of the severe lasting damage he is doing himself by his defiance.[20]

17. Galatians 1.16.

18. Acts 9.4, 22.7.

19. Pindar, *Pythian Odes* 2.95, Euripides, *Bacchanals* 795, Aeschylus, *Agamemnon* 1624. In Psalms of Solomon 16.4, God steers man away from the wrong path by pricking him as a rider does his horse: a very different thing.

20. According to J. Munck, *Acts of the Apostles*, rev. W. F. Albright and C. S. Mann, 1967, p. 242, the clause deals with the future: 'from now on it will be difficult for you to kick against the goad', 'the call of Christ will from now on constrain you'. This sounds too abrupt after 'Why do you persecute me?', which is about the past and present. Again, future recalcitrance is so out of the question that there is no need to enlarge on its futility. Lastly—a decisive objection—the text ought to contain some pointer at least to 'from now on' if we were intended to take it that way.

Acts 22.16 tells us how, as soon as his sight was restored, his instructor exhorted him: 'And now, why do you tarry? Arise and be baptized'. To take the first clause as a mere jovial encouragement cannot be right, considering the overwhelming significance of the situation. It must be a condemnation of the slightest traces of holding off. While the circumstances could not be more different from those relating to the King of Adiabene, it is less remote from 'How long will you continue uncircumcised?' than might appear at first sight.

I Corinthians 15.8 brings out the point most strongly. 'But last of all he was seen also of me, as of one born out of due time'.[21]

Of three Septuagintal occurrences of *ektroma*, two need not detain us. The stricken Job wishes never to have lived, to be like 'an untimely birth coming out of the womb, infants who never saw the light'; and Ecclesiastes laments that, however blessed a man may be with children and long life, if he cannot enjoy it, 'an untimely birth is better than he, for it comes in vain and goes in darkness and has not seen the sun'.[22] In the straits here contemplated, to be 'an untimely birth' is a good thing whereas normally, and in I Corinthians, it is about the worst. The third text is all the more important. It is from the Pentateuch, from Num-

21. I gratefully borrow from the literature, in particular J. D. Schneider, art. '*ektroma*', in *Theologisches Wörterbuch zum Neuen Testament*, ed. G. Kittel, 1935, 2:463ff.; H. Lietzmann, *An die Korinther I/II*, 4th ed. by W. G. Kümmel, 1979, pp. 78, 192; C. K. Barrett, *The First Epistle to the Corinthians*, 1968, pp. 343ff.; W. F. Orr and J. A. Walther, *I Corinthians*, 1976, pp. 318, 322f.; G. W. E. Nickelsburg, 'An *ektroma*, Though Appointed from the Womb: Paul's Apostolic Self-Description in 1 Corinthians 15 and Galatians 1', in *Essays in Honor of Krister Stendahl*, pp. 198ff. All of these authors mention other important contributions.

22. Job 3.16, Ecclesiastes 6.3. See my 'Black Hole', in *Rechtshistorisches Journal* 2 (1983): 182ff.

bers,[23] part of an amazing interlude—amazing at least to
readers two thousand years or so ago. Miriam is struck
with leprosy for maligning Moses, and Aaron, her accom-
plice, asks Moses to get her healed: 'May she not be as
something equal to death, as an untimely birth coming out
of the mother's womb, and it consumes half of her flesh'. It
is this precedent on which Paul bases and which would occur to such recipients of his letter as were at all in touch
with Scripture.

To get an idea of the speculation the episode engendered,
we need only survey the ancient versions and expositions of
this very line. The underlying Hebrew includes no noun
'untimely birth' at all and, indeed, is altogether much
plainer: 'May she not be as the dead one that, when he
comes out of his mother's womb, half of his flesh is consumed'. What led to the Greek is far from obvious. Perhaps, in the translator's judgment, the crass likening of
Miriam to a corpse sounded implausible or even irreligious.
He resorted to elaboration, thereby introducing the rare
term—by which he may understand a live monsterbirth.
This does not, however, account for a switch at the end:
while the Hebrew speaks of the dead child's devastation,
the Septuagint speaks of the mother's, 'half of her flesh'.
No doubt the child's is taken for granted; even so, the addition of the mother remains baffling. Philo, incidentally, in
his *Allegorical Interpretation*,[24] takes over *ektroma* and follows
the Greek also in assuming harm to the mother. One cer-
tainty that emerges is that already in the epoch of the Septuagint this incident was eagerly studied.

To proceed to Aramaic, Onkelos eliminates anything
smacking of a person's death, be it fetus or adult. 'May she
not be removed from our midst [the camp] since she is our

23. Numbers 12.12.
24. 1.24.76.

sister; pray now over this dead flesh being in her and she will be healed'. By contrast, the Jerusalemite Targum describes her as a leper 'unclean in her tent as one dead' and at great length compares her to a child that completes nine months in the womb and perishes as the mother is sitting down on the travailing chair: Miriam went with the rest through the trials of Egypt and the desert but, unless restored, is to be banished now that they are approaching their land.

Like the Septuagint, the Siphre interferes with 'his flesh'. It does not, of course, alter the wording but it argues that its real meaning is 'our flesh', in the sense of 'our sister'; and by similarly interpreting 'his mother' as 'our mother', it achieves a result close to Onkelos. Aaron's plea to Moses, that is, must be understood thus: 'May she not be unclean like one dead, she who came out of the womb of our mother, so that [if nothing is done about it] half of our sister is consumed'.[25]

It would lead too far afield to set forth, however summarily, the mighty and subtle thoughts massed in this brief narrative, all of them again and again drawn on by future Biblical authors.[26] Here are the features which explain why Paul has recourse to it. Its bête noir is a prophetess who badly falls down on her vocation, inveighing against the God-appointed leader, in fact, the precursor of the Messiah to come. No one deserves such an attack less: he is 'very meek, above all the men that are on the face of the earth'.

25. Needless to say, the Siphre feels justified in redirecting the pronoun: Aaron is displaying such reverence towards Moses that he will not dare to say 'our', as if they were comrades. See K. G. Kuhn, *Sifre zu Numeri*, 1933–1934, pp. 224, 275.

26. An inter-testamental quotation: Sirach 45.4, 'For his faithfulness and meekness he chose him out of all flesh'. A New Testament one: Hebrews 3.2, 'As also Moses was faithful in all his house'.

This, though he far surpasses the ordinary prophet: 'My servant Moses, in all my house he is trusted, mouth to mouth will I speak with him'. When the Lord threatens her with condign horrendous punishment, with for ever being 'as an *ektroma*', it is her innocent victim whose prayer saves her. Not from some discipline: she has to bear with shameful seclusion for a period. But even this is lightened by the people patiently waiting for her instead of marching on; lightened and at the same time rendered more deplorable, since the communal goal will be reached that much later. That Paul would detect in this drama an anticipation of his destiny is small wonder—on the presupposition that, despite baptism, he continues answerable for his extended, bitter fight against it.

Not a few questions I shall leave open. For instance, when he confesses to 'having persecuted the church of God', is this an echo—in part—of the hurt to the mother in the Septuagint and Philo? Again, does *ektroma* in his Epistle denote a fetus miscarried—the usual sense of the noun—or one stillborn—the case envisaged in the Jerusalemite Targum—or a live monsterbirth—possibly alluded to by the Septuagint? Maybe one should not even try to pin him down. Yet harder is the following: is he distressed chiefly by his No to the task laid on him from conception or to that he learned about from those like Stephen sent to enlighten him? Whichever line we take, the designation from Numbers, where it brings out the abject fate of the leper, evokes a child gruesomely disfigured as it emerges from the mother. Paul is that child. He, 'the last', missed being around the human Jesus or finding his way into the church at its dawn. Instead, those lost years were exceptionally unfortunate, marked not merely by a holding back but by the grossest misdeeds. Such contumacy towards his deeper, better knowledge leaves him mutilated and penitent even now.

In conclusion, I retract what I said above about his never hinting that baptism has made the crooked straight. Paradoxically and providentially, it is just the hellish attribute he owns up to which implies relief. Miriam, his predecessor, obtained forgiveness through the mediation of the holy one whom she had persecuted. Not without having to expiate by accepting pain and disgrace—but still, full forgiveness in the end. So it will be with him. His identifying with her, by the way, is yet another item that should weigh in assessing the place of women in his anthropology. It would not, indeed, be surprising if she were in his mind in another section of the same Epistle, equally dealing with a legend from Numbers—the Israelites drinking of the rock that accompanied them. The Rabbis call this rock 'Miriam's well'.[27]

27. I Corinthians 10.4, Numbers 20.7ff., 21.16ff. The first named Rabbi mentioning it is Hiyya, around A.D. 200, Palestinian Kilaim 32c. But that he is not coining a novel concept may be inferred both from the way he speaks and from first-century statements like Joshua's, Mekhilta on Exodus 16.35, and Pseudo-Philo's, *Antiquities* 21A. For more texts, see H. L. Strack and P. Billerbeck, *Kommentar zum Neuen Testament aus Talmud und Midrasch*, 4 vols., 1924–1929, rept. 1969, passim.

Appeasing or Resisting the Oppressor

I

Probably you expect some advice on how to handle University Chancellors or Law School Deans. But I shall talk on a more sombre subject which has overshadowed a large part of my life: the choice between appeasement and resistance if you belong to a group under the rule of another one fiercely hostile and with absolute power. My main discussion will focus on events of one and a half to two millennia ago; some guidelines from Jewish experience at various stages of Roman supremacy are still worth pondering.

To ease you into the atmosphere of this field, let me begin with a personal reminiscence. I live with a woman[1]

To Ernst Bammel—since 1955—and his wife Caroline. At the beginning of last academic year, my colleagues Michael E. Smith and Philippe Nonet suggested that I deliver a special lecture at Boalt Hall and, joined by Sanford Kadish, made the arrangements. It came off on 19 February 1986. I wish to express my gratitude to them for a, to me, wonderful occasion.

1. Between delivery and publication of this address we got married.

with whom I have never won an argument. Once only I came close and even then was routed. Here is what happened. Soon after World War II, in 1948 or '49—years before I knew her—I was lunching in a Strasbourg restaurant with friends. It was a lively place. Yet all conversation came to a sudden halt as the door opened and three elderly men walked in, one of them obviously central. This reverential hush lasted till well after they had sat down at a table. Then, gradually, people started talking again. I asked my companions for the meaning, and the following story emerged. During the occupation of the city, in retaliation for an act of sabotage, the Commandant of the occupying troops sent out a detachment to conduct a *razzia*; that is to say, the soldiers sealed off four or five blocks downtown, picked up there any males who looked like between fifteen and fifty and took them to the courtyard of headquarters—where they were to be shot. As it chanced, the two sons of the dignitary—ex-Mayor or the like—who had just entered were walking together in the area and got arrested. Somebody immediately informed him. He gained access to the Commandant, the window of whose office in fact gave out to the yard with the twelve or so victims already lined up for the firing. He set forth his plight. The Commandant, nonchalantly waving towards the window, said: 'All right, you can have one of them'. But he could not bring himself to act on this direction and both were executed. It was that drama, my hosts explained, which accounted for the reaction of the lunchers.

When, in the early seventies, I reported this to Helen, she—then at the height of her psychoanalytic venture—did not acclaim the protagonist. He deserved pity, she held, but not homage. He was made a cruel offer, to be sure. But he declined it, not from love of his sons or for the sake of their welfare, but selfishly, because he was afraid of the guilt he would feel later towards the one abandoned to die. The truly heroic thing would have been to act as instructed and then cope, or maybe fail to cope, with the pangs of self-reproach. Certainly his response was very understandable and, yes, meriting compassion, but not admiration. Well, she put this to me of an evening, when I am generally not so good at sustained reasoning with her. As usual, I recovered in the morning, on my way from North Beach to Boalt Hall, and I sensed something off in her thesis. Those people in the café were not all taken in by what would be, basically, an evasion of responsibility. Soon it became clear to me that what they honoured was a refusal of collaboration. By accepting, the petitioner would have involved himself in the entire operation of which, indeed, this sideshow would be a particularly ugly part, bringing out to the full the arbitrary playing with human life.

Before stepping down from my bus, I had worked out to my satisfaction solid proof that it must be his rejection of the tyrant's lure, at enormous cost, which moved the Strasbourgers. Contrast the following case, alike in all respects but this one. A father strolls along the shore with his two children, aged six and four. An unexpected wave sweeps both into the sea. He may just be able to rescue one. If he remains passive because he cannot make up his mind between them, the situation does approximate Helen's assessment; and we shall pity him but not pay him homage. What is the difference? It is that here the calamity is due to a force of nature when, normally, we do our best and deal with the consequences as they unfold. The Strasbourg father was faced by a devilish man-made scheme; and, rather than participate, he sacrificed his progeny. Had the stroller who lost his babes to the ocean appeared at the restaurant, there might well have been some manifestation of sympathy but not conceivably that profound awe. Back with Helen at the end of the day, I expounded it all. She listened—which she does not always do—but what did she say? 'Yes, that is correct. But a mother would have taken one home with her'.

She is right, of course. Those soundly, nobly motivated objections to ever doing business with Satan are, au fond, of a political nature, the ultimate aim being to ensure decent government. In a conflict between such principles and concrete, close, personal bonds, the latter, for women—those not turned into men at any rate—take precedence. Even that abominable thing, collaboration, is outer, means nothing compared with the inner, the immediate, natural tie. Though, for once, having to strike the flag of the mind, she hoisted in its place the more stirring one of the heart. The public at the restaurant was predominantly male. I shall briefly come back to the feminine approach at the close, when adverting to a Marxist one which now and then looks deceptively similar.

A rider about this episode, however, should be added. I have long come to realize that its star ought not to be idolized. How did he get to be warned of what was going on without a moment's delay? A graver question: how did he get to be admitted to the enemy chief, and in the midst of a precarious exploit? Plainly, he had dubious connections. Again, what was the purpose of his visit? To save his sons. Ergo: he would happily have gone off with them, leaving the other innocents to perish; at best, he might feel sorry for them. His anti-collaborationist impulse was triggered by having a ghastly dilemma forced upon him. Still, let us not be too hard: we most of us are not saints ourselves. For that matter, who knows?, besides all the malevolence in the Commandant's proposal there may have been a flicker of mercy.

II

Moving back now in history, the problem before the Rabbis I shall concentrate on was: what ought a collective—a town, a congregation—to do if the reigning power, enraged maybe by signs of insubordination, or for the fun of it, orders it, say, to hand over that same day three members for public hanging; in the event of defiance, the entire community or half of it or sixty persons will be wiped out. I have published a little tract on this topic.[1] At the time, I bracketed out the relevant New Testament material, reserving it for subsequent consideration.[2] Today is my opportunity.

The initial Pharisaic stand—I shall deal with the Sadducees further on—was unbendingly negative: no one to be surrendered ever, even though extinction will ensue. Clearly, no such scruples are entertained by the Judeans in Judges who, fearing what their mighty Philistine neighbours might do to settle accounts with the indomitable Samson, propose to deliver him up in fetters. It is only his

1. *Collaboration with Tyranny in Rabbinic Law*, 1965. The chief texts are Mishnah Terumoth 8.12, Tosephta Terumoth 7.20, Jerusalemite Terumoth 46b, Genesis Rabba 94 on 46.26f. E. J. Schochet supplements them by medieval ones in his searching treatise *A Responsum of Surrender*, 1973, an edition and analysis of a sixteenth-century Rabbinic advice on a tragic case in Poland. A summary was already furnished in his *Bach = Rabbi Joel Sirkes*, 1971, p. 132.

2. *Collaboration with Tyranny*, p. 18. John Noonan complained at once. E. Bammel has inspected the New Testament side, first in a review in *Theologische Literaturzeitung* 93 (1968): 833ff., then in a major paper, 'Ex illa itaque die consilium fecerunt . . .', in *The Trial of Jesus, Cambridge Studies in Honour of C. F. D. Moule*, ed. E. Bammel, 1970, pp. 11ff. While alive to the strength of his argumentation, I differ in my general approach. A rough overview may be found in my *Civil Disobedience in Antiquity*, 1972, pp. 97ff. Huge gaps remain. If, twenty years hence, Michael, Philippe and Sandy desire an encore, I shall try to assess Josephus's contribution to this terrain. For a minuscule specimen see below, under V, footnote 21.

giant strength lent him by the Lord that saves him.[3] A proper ruling was first formulated with regard to heathen thugs asking a company of travellers to let them have one for killing (for having sport with him, would be a likely sixteenth-century euphemism) otherwise they will kill the lot; an astonishing variant of this collision in the Old Testament will be presented in due course.[4] A demand by the Roman masters, the Pharisees contend, is no better. The dogma may indeed have hastened the outbreak of the war against them in A.D. 66. Florus, the procurator, ordered the Jewish leaders of Jerusalem to give up a number of men who had abused him in public; he was told that it was impossible to identify them; whereupon he had his soldiers sack the 'upper market', three thousand six hundred persons were slaughtered and chances for a settlement rapidly vanished.[5]

Scriptural support was found in Deuteronomy, which makes it a capital crime to sell a fellow-Jew, scil. to abroad. More precisely, it condemns sale of 'any of your brothers, the children of Israel', the redundant 'your brothers' no doubt alluding to the saga of Joseph, sold to the Ishmaelites by his brothers literally.[6] For the Rabbis, in this context, to deliver up a person in return for safety is a selling just as much as if it were done for money. The ruling prevailed both before A.D. 70, while a measure of self-government remained under Roman suzerainty, and for several decennia after.

It became untenable, however, in the Hadrianic persecu-

---

3. Judges 15.9ff.

4. See below, under V, item 5.

5. Josephus, *Jewish War* 2.14.8.301ff.

6. Deuteronomy 24.7. See C. Carmichael, *The Laws of Deuteronomy*, 1974, pp. 212ff., *Law and Narrative in the Bible*, 1985, pp. 261f., 305.

tion following the defeat of Bar-Kochba in 135, when circumcision, Sabbath services, religious instruction were in-
terdicted on pain of death. That these activities continued
underground goes without saying, and the Romans went
all out to stop them. To go on rigidly disregarding an ultimatum of theirs of the kind in question would in no time
have put an end—really an end, no metaphor—to Palestinian Jewry, decimated already. Accordingly, at a secret synod
of the Sages, the majority established a distinction. If the
authorities request an unnamed victim or number of victims—let us have one or five of you to be executed, or else
you will all go—the old maxim applies: the answer is No.
However, if they specify—give us Avrom or Avrom, Ba-
ruch and Gedaliah—they are to be obeyed. The former
demand is utterly barbarous, treating humans like cattle,
fungibles. A secondary objection is that the selection is im-
posed on the community and, whatever procedure it might
resort to, trust would be undermined—not to speak of the
inevitable burden of guilt. (Volunteers cannot solve the
problem, but I shall not go into detail.) Obliteration is
better than descent to this level. The latter demand evinces
a glimmer of justice, being for someone they have a quarrel
with: even if they want a pious scholar because he has
taught Torah, at least he is not simply an object replaceable
by any other of the same description. Neither will there be
the evil selection by the group. Here, then, though the
price is horrendous, it may be paid to ensure survival of the
whole. (I suppose, under this formula, the head of a congregation of three hundred in 1943, notified to have ready
by next morning twenty of them for a transport to exter-
mination, otherwise everybody will be despatched, had to
refuse; ordered to have ready twenty designated persons
who had contributed to pacifist journals, he had to yield.
What about the dread predicament in Bosic's *The Judge*?)
The Biblical text invoked in favour of this concession was

the narrative of Sheba, a rebel against King David. David's
general prepared to storm the city in which he was holding
out but offered peace if he were delivered up to him. The
residents did toss his head over the wall and the general
withdrew: surrender of a named person for the sake of the
universality.[7] Evidently, the use of this precedent implied a
degree of recognition of Roman rule.

A minority declined to budge. Deuteronomy's was the
only right way. Jewry would not go under: God could work
a miracle at any time and his people should move him to do
so by a sincere return. As for Sheba, he defected from the
legitimate, heaven-appointed sovereign, nothing to do with
the foreign usurpers. It is worth observing that the two factions of the synod were agreed that an individual, threatened with death unless he kills someone, unnamed or named,
must choose death—actually, irrespective of whether the
other is Jewish or not.[8] The limitation to 'any of the children of Israel' does not here apply.

By the third century, the danger had abated and the
trend was towards greater firmness. This comes out clearly
in a case giving rise to a legend. A Jew sought by the Romans[9] for what must have been something like terrorism
was given shelter by a leading Rabbi at Lydda. It should be
noticed right away—in view of what will follow—that,
palpably, the Rabbi was risking his life. The Romans found
out that the criminal was hiding in that city and proclaimed
that, unless he was handed over, it would be sacked. At this
the Rabbi persuaded his guest to willingly accept his fate.
So much for the case: here legend takes over. Up to this
incident, the prophet Elijah had paid regular visits to the
Rabbi, so they might exchange news about goings-on in

7. II Samuel 20.
8. Jerusalemite Sanhedrin 21b, Babylonian Sanhedrin 74a.
9. Or, less probably, by Zenobia, Queen of Palmyra.

paradise and on earth. Now the visits stopped. The Rabbi, disconsolate, prayed and fasted and finally Elijah returned. Asked why he had stayed away, he replied that he did not use to consort with betrayers—the term is familiar from the deed of Judas, *masar, paradidomi*. The Rabbi defended himself by citing the resolution of the synod. But Elijah declared that those truly devout would not follow that teaching. Strong criticism, and it is not surprising—at this junction we return to reality—that before long another influential scholar advocated a mighty limitation to the synod's concession: even a specific person claimed by the alien power may be transferred only if he is actually deserving of death. (By this criterion, the pacifist journalists were not to be turned over.) The Biblical Sheba, after all, was guilty of armed high treason. Unless the condition is satisfied, the community must allow itself to be slaughtered. The requirement foreshadows modern extradition clauses, but I shall not expand.[10]

Virtually no room is left in the Rabbinic deliberations for the possibility that, now and then, it might be from genuine moderation or even sympathy that a collective is called on to give up a member in order to avoid worse. Whereas, for instance, in Second Samuel's original recital of the Sheba affair, this aspect predominates. Joab is here portrayed as fully concurring with the wise woman who interceded for the city. Though it had abetted the revolt, it remained a sacred constituent of the nation, and he would be dismayed if, because he could not otherwise get hold of the leader, he had to go to extremes. The reason for the difference is that the warring factions of Second Samuel were

10. Below, under V, item 4, we shall find the Danaides begging for sanctuary at Argos, and the king taking pains to discover whether they are in the right. See my brother Benjamin's *Zu den Rechtsproblemen in Aischylos' Agamemnon*, 1938, pp. 78ff.

still linked by strong, old bonds.[11] Not so those here under review. The Rabbis had little cause for thinking that a Roman commander, involved in a serious conflict with the Jews, would ever feel protectively about a community of theirs.

Of course, the high standards of the Sages were not always practised. In the Middle Ages, in particular, in many places sad breakdowns in spirit occurred. A frightened congregation would regard the slightest misbehaviour of a member in the outer world as menacing its existence—not without reason. Motivation mattered little: in fact, one acting from religious zeal was likely to do it again, hence a special threat, a troublemaker. He might be offered up almost before the authorities turned nasty. (There is a foretaste as early as during the serfdom in Egypt).[12] Still, we have plenty of evidence of a collective, however pressured, faithfully approaching a respected Rabbi for guidance; e.g. when, in 1620, a Kalish Jew was charged with stealing the host,[13] or even from the period of World War II.

III

Who stands where? The patricians incline to accommodation, their less attached colleagues to going through

11. According to C. Carmichael, 'On Deuteronomic Legislation—Sparing the Mother Bird', *Law and History Review* 2 (1984): 288ff., Deuteronomy 22.6f. alludes to this campaign. If he is right, as I think he is, the lawgiver evidently sees there a worthy compromise: the mother, the city as a whole, is to be let off, and with this proviso, it is quite in order to dispose of undeserving nestlings such as the renegade. None of this is incompatible with my conjectures in *Ancient Jewish Law*, 1981, pp. 99f., but such refinements can wait.

12. Exodus 5.21.

13. See Schochet, *Responsum of Surrender*.

with it. The majority opinion of the assembly during the Hadrianic terror—viz. that to escape annihilation, a community should sacrifice a member specifically targeted by the government—was propounded by Judah ben Ilai, son of a famous father, an admirer of Roman civilisation, in the end awarded an honour by the Romans. The minority's spokesman, Simeon ben Johai, was a mystic, despised Rome and for many years lived with a price on his head. Nor should we overlook a personal hurt: it was an insider's denunciation which led to his being outlawed. And another: quite possibly, his own father's sympathies and even activities were in flagrant contrast with his.[1] In the next century, Joshua ben Levi, reproved by Elijah, was president of the academy of Lydda, wealthy, on good terms with the proconsul. Similarly, the slightly younger Johanan, who also upheld that majority ruling, was president of the academy of Tiberias and traced his descent back to the pre-exilic epoch. By contrast, we know nothing about the ancestry of Resh Laqish who, by barring any extradition incompatible with justice, virtually preached return to defiance regardless of the consequences. High as he rose, he was never allowed to forget about his adolescence in abject poverty, when he sold himself as gladiator and acquired plebeian habits for good. (Elijah sided with the idealists: the saints in heaven always do that.) It would be simplistic to rush to judgment as to the relative merits, practical or moral, of the two camps; I hope my gut response is not too noticeable. Fortunately, for the purpose in hand, it is enough to locate them.

This brings me to the Sadducees, the aristocrats par excellence—and, indeed, they did anticipate the compromisers among the Pharisees by at least one hundred years. At some stage, Jesus's activity alarmed the more cautious

1. Babylonian Shabbath 33b f., Pesahim 112a. His son stood by him.

ones of his compatriots: it seemed about to drive the Romans into 'intervening and taking away the place and the nation', into clamping down, that is, by paganizing the Temple and suppressing what self-government endured.[2] The attribution of this misgiving to 'the chief priests and the Pharisees' sounds very plausible: the former would enlist as many of the latter as they could. (This kind of conscription is common throughout history. An efficient elite knows when it needs the backing of numbers. I have watched striking instances in my life, among states, among parties within a state, among strata within a denomination, a city, a university and so forth).[3] Admittedly, there was no formal ultimatum threatening physical extirpation. But if what was feared came to pass, thousands of Jews would die and the loss of the Temple would be almost worse. Remember Philo's defence, less than ten years later, of the Judaeans preparing for collective suicide should Caligula put up a statue of himself in the sanctuary.[4] Viewed thus, therefore, it was the life of a specific zealot versus the future of the entire body, and the high priest Caiaphas argued that 'one man should die for the people and the whole nation perish not'.[5] He was a Sadducee, scion of an eminent dynasty, appointed not by the Jews but by Valerius Gratus, predecessor of Pontius Pilate. He took the line then to which the major-

2. John 11.48.

3. The corresponding phenomenon in reverse is the support a struggling subjugated group receives from wayward members of the governing one—saints, traitors, mavericks. The patrician Appius Claudius enabled a son of one of his freedmen to publish the secret archives of the pontiffs; Livy, *From the Founding of the City* 9.46.7ff.

4. *Embassy to Gaius* 32.229ff. See my *Civil Disobedience in Antiquity*, pp. 92ff., and 'Three Footnotes on Civil Disobedience in Antiquity', *Humanities in Society* 2 (1979): 79f.

5. John 11.50, 18.14.

ity of Pharisaic leaders found themselves reduced under Hadrian. One of the two sources relating the end of Ullah actually has Joshua ben Levi remind him that 'it is better to kill that man [= you] so they may not punish the congregation on his [= your] account'.[6] Whether this detail is authentic or not,[7] it does underscore the identity of the synod's position with that of Caiaphas.

Fundamentally, the entanglement was nothing new. Long before, in the second third of the second century B.C., Alcinus, a Hellenizer, elevated to the high-priesthood by the Syrian king, had abetted the latter's fight against the Hasmonaean rebels. The king's general ordered the Temple personnel, whom he knew to loathe Alcinus and be hand in glove with the rebels despite their outward subservience, to hand over Judas Maccabaeus. They swore they were ignorant of his whereabouts; whereupon he, infuriated, told them that unless they handed him over, their Temple would be replaced by one to Dionysos after victory. Well, he was defeated.[8]

That Caiaphas was opposing the original, inflexible Pharisaic No is reflected in his angry language: 'You know nothing'. Furthermore, he called the abandonment of the person who imperiled them all 'expedient', 'beneficial', *symphero*. The term—of enormous importance in Paul—characterizes conduct deviating from hallowed principle,

6. Genesis Rabba 94 on 46.26f.

7. In all likelihood, alas, it is something in between: the maxim as such comes down from the beginning of the Christian era via inner-Jewish transmission—not the New Testament, that is—but is put into Joshua ben Levi's mouth after the event. Had he quoted it, it is difficult to see why it would have been dropped by the Jerusalemite Talmud.

8. I Maccabees 7.6ff., II Maccabees 14.3ff., Josephus, *Jewish Antiquities* 12.10.1.389ff.

yet the decidedly superior one because of special circumstances. As things stood, he protested, it was misguided to
make a fetish even of a warning with roots so deep in the
past as Deuteronomy's against sale of an Israelite. This indeed explains the notable feature, that with not one syllable
does he criticize the substance of Jesus's words or deeds:
he argues entirely from *raison d'état*, from the overriding,
public-necessity–geared reservation to the hard line. Quite
likely, the Sadducees already in that period referred to
Sheba in corroboration.[9] When Caiaphas exclaimed, 'You
do not consider, *logizomai*, that it is expedient' etc., he may
well have used the verb in the sense of 'to draw the proper
conclusions from the ancient reports'. At any rate, this account of his outlook belongs to the invaluable, historical
items preserved by John alone.

(Re a twist in the end of Sheba. The appeasers invoked
his treatment in support of their readiness to hand over a
wanted person to the enemy if the alternative was extirpation of the group. Yet he was not strictly handed over, or
better, was handed over only in an over-literal sense: Joab's
request was satisfied by the citizens themselves cutting off
his quarry's head and throwing it out to him—which had
the advantage that none of the besiegers entered the place.
The use made of the case is not, however, hard to understand. In most such confrontations, the tyrant would mind
as little as Joab whether the individual he was after was surrendered or despatched on the spot; and quite reasonably,
the Sages judged the latter a selling, a handing over, no less
than the former. The narrow interrelation of the two modes
of knuckling under is amply evidenced—not least in New
Testament times. What chiefly worried Herod Antipas

9. I had not gotten this far in my analysis when surmising—
Collaboration with Tyranny, p. 60—that it was probably Judah ben
Ilai who first held him up as illustrating a reservation to the taboo
on sale.

about the Baptist's near-seditious activity may well have been the Roman reaction to be expected; so he ordered his execution.[10] At some stage, to go by Luke,[11] he had the same intention with regard to Jesus, but eventually found it politic to leave the final deed to the occupying power, handing him over *stricto sensu*. As for John,[12] in the first Caiaphas session, chief priests and Pharisees determined to kill Jesus—presumably somehow or other, themselves or through a convenient agency. As things developed, they saw to his arrest but got the Romans to crucify him: again, an actual handing over. The Sages were realistic in having the precedent from Samuel cover all these situations.)

The evangelist adds a Christological interpretation: owing to divine dispensation, the high priest's utterance constituted a prophecy that Jesus would indeed die for the best, 'die for the nation, and not for the nation only but in order that he might gather together into one the children of God that were scattered'.[13] Here the archetypal victim of the transaction outlawed by Deuteronomy is directly introduced: Jesus becomes a second, ultimate Joseph. The latter, reunited with his brothers, comforts them: 'God sent me ahead of you to preserve life', scil. among the heathens, in a famine, 'and to save your lives', scil. the chosen band.[14] Again, 'God brought it to pass to save much people alive', referring to the Egyptians, and 'Now I will nourish you and your little ones', referring to his kin.[15] The near-technical term, it should be observed, recurs in Jesus's farewell: 'It is expedient, beneficial, for you that I go away'.[16]

---

10. Josephus, *Jewish Antiquities* 18.5.2.117ff. No doubt personal rancune, of the sort brought out in the Synoptics (Matthew 14.3ff., Mark 6.17ff., Luke 3.19f.), was also involved.

11. 13.31, 23.11ff.   12. 11.53, 10.12ff.

13. John 11.51f.   14. Genesis 45.5ff.

15. Genesis 50.20f.   16. John 16.7.

IV

Obviously, from the moment of his arrest, Jesus must have reminded people of Joseph[1]—not only the learned few acquainted with the latter's place in the discussion of relations with the outside world but also the unlearned many. As Joseph was disposed of by his real brothers, so Jesus was by one as good as a brother. What is more, his mercenary seller bore the same name as that brother of Joseph who instigated the deed, recommending it as more lucrative than an outright killing would be.[2] Some ancient exegetes do draw the inference that Judah thereby forfeited his privileged rank;[3] presumably this viewpoint was once more widespread than would appear from the sources, on the whole preferring to exonerate him. (To be fair, a later test proved him resolved to bear heavy vicarious affliction: he begged to be enslaved instead of Benjamin when Joseph—not as yet having disclosed who he was—proposed to keep the latter for the theft of the cup found in his sack while permitting the others to return to Canaan.)[4] One might indeed wonder whether the name of the New Testament traitor is not an imaginative transfer from the Old. I think there is good reason—not here to be set

1. Genesis 37.18ff., Matthew 10.4, 26.14ff., 21ff., 45ff., 27.3ff., Mark 14.10f., 18ff., 41ff., Luke 22.3ff., 21ff., 47ff., John 13.2ff., 21ff., 18.2ff. In my *New Testament and Rabbinic Judaism*, 1956, rept. 1973, pp. 3f., the role of Joseph is grossly underrated. I so strove to be cautious that the result was as wrong in one direction as overkill would have made it in the other.

2. Genesis 37.26f.

3. Genesis Rabba 85 on 38.1, Exodus Rabba 42 on 32.7.

4. Genesis 44.17ff. This is a rough statement: no need here to enter into the exact function of the offer in the mind of the cycle's author.

out[5]—for refraining from this conclusion. Anyhow, if we did have to do with a nickname (by now it definitely has become one), that would only strengthen my case for an immediate, general recognition of the parallel.

Let me add one more coincidence. Simeon ben Johai's violent propaganda came to the knowledge of the authorities through a favourite disciple, son of proselytes—whose name was Judah. And, for good measure, a dysincidence: you will have noted that it was the Maccabean Judas whom the foreign invader sought to get betrayed—yes, *paradidomi*.

Once the catastrophe was mastered, another analogy would be readily seen: in both cases a despicable wrong opened the road to triumph—to exodus, Sinai and the land in the one, redemption in the other. It is in fact this feature of Joseph's biography, its pointing far beyond itself, which radically distinguishes it from otherwise comparable Near Eastern commemorations of marvellous losings and findings. It is taken up in the Psalter: 'He [God] sent ahead of them a man, as a slave was sold Joseph. . . . And there came Israel to Egypt. . . . And he sent Moses . . . and he brought them out . . . and he gave them the lands of the nations'.[6] An *Ur*-Christian brought up in this milieu could hardly miss the link to the present renewal.

John, however, goes much further with his elaborate filling in of Messianic features. (Nothing like it in the other evangelists, except for an isolated pericope towards the beginning of Luke.)[7] When he dwells on the overarching

5. W. R. Farmer's comments on naming in that era are pertinent. In *Maccabees, Zealots and Josephus*, 1956, p. viii, he writes: 'Then I noticed how frequently the leaders of seditious activity against Rome bore the same names as the early Maccabees—Mattathias, Judas, John, Eleazar, Jonathan, Simon'.

6. Psalms 105.17ff.

7. Luke 2.41ff.; see Appendix below. The way I hear John is greatly indebted to C. K. Barrett's seminal study 'The Old Testa-

plan which the evildoers help to accomplish and which, in fact, makes their most abject wickedness result in the greatest blessing—to cite just Jesus's reply to the governor: 'You could have no power against me except it were given you from above'[8]—the specific texts about Joseph are among his stimuli. 'It was not you that sent me hither but God'. 'You thought evil against me, but God meant it unto good'.[9] It has been contended that Paul, in Romans and Galatians, and John, in his Gospel and the First Epistle, independently accord centrality to 'the Saviour sent in order that he perform his function': they must be drawing, therefore, on a primitive credal formula.[10] A drawing on the Joseph paradigm is an alternative and, at least as far as John is concerned, preferable explanation, the tone is so alike. Joseph: 'God sent me ahead of you for [the furtherance of] life'.[11] Fourth Gospel: 'God sent his son in order that the world should be saved', immediately following upon 'God gave his son in order that every believer should have eternal life'[12]—near enough though with 'to give' in the place of 'to send'. First Epistle: 'God sent his son in order that we should live', 'God sent his son as propitiation', 'God sent his son as saviour'.[13] I shall not speculate about a credal formula itself inspired by the miracle in Egypt: too remote a chance.

(It is true that Joseph's statement contains no 'in order that', but the emergence of this construction in the New Testament is easily accounted for by its generally increasing

---

ment in the Fourth Gospel', *Journal of Theological Studies* 48 (1947): 155ff.

8. John 19.11. Samson's story, adverted to above, II, footnote 3, is also in point.

9. Genesis 45.8, 50.20.

10. John 3.17, Romans 8.3, Galatians 4.4, I John 4.9f., 14. See M. Hengel, *Der Sohn Gottes*, 1975, p. 24.

11. Genesis 45.5.   12. John 3.16f.   13. I John 4.9f., 14.

popularity.[14] As a matter of fact, two of the pertinent verses in the First Epistle themselves do without it[15] even though, overall, John is affected by the general trend to an extraordinary degree.[16] One difficulty with the other thesis is[17] that Paul, though earlier than John, defines the mission in far more doctrinal fashion, as purposing a higher fulfilment of the law or a ransoming of those under the law. John speaks of to save, to live, propitiation, saviour. With the exception of propitiation—mentioned to remind us how the life celebrated in the previous sentence was made possible— this is all quite basic, and close to the Old Testament. A second objection: 'to send' appears as *pempo* in Romans, *exapostello* in Galatians. They are near-synonymous but, if a credal profession were underlying, one would expect no switch. The three passages from John claimed to base on the creed all employ *apostello*—employed as in Genesis; and in the psalm just cited, too, it is *apostello* or *exapostello*. Lastly, in Romans, 'in order that' is not really attached to 'to send' but to 'to condemn': 'God, having sent his son, condemned sin in the flesh in order that the higher law be fulfilled after the spirit'.)

   That so sensitive a typologist should be captivated by those passages in the old narrative is to be expected. Here, within a minimal space—about three verses—are clustered these tremendous slogans of salvation history: 'God sends' a saviour from his home to a distant populace, for 'to keep alive a multitude of people' among the latter and 'maintain

14. See F. Blass and A. Debrunner, *Grammatik des neutestamentlichen Griechisch*, 14th ed. by F. Rehkopf, 1976, pp. 314ff.

15. I John 4.10, 'God sent his son as propitiation', 4.14, 'as saviour'.

16. E.g. John 1.27, 4.34. See W. Bauer, *Das Johannesevangelium*, 2d ed., 1925, pp. 32, 69.

17. As pointed out by Hengel himself; and I agree with him that it is by no means fatal.

a remnant' among his own, destined for 'a great deliverance'. ('Multitude', 'much', *rabh* in Hebrew, *polys* in Greek, often approaches an idealistic 'all';[18] it may do so here, and if not, many a devout student will have assumed this sense. Amos hopes God will be gracious to 'the remnant of Joseph'.[19] 'Remnant' and 'deliverance'—or other formations from these two roots—are coupled in a fair number of significant texts: 'From Jerusalem shall go out a remnant and a deliverance from mount Zion'.[20]) The whole of it set in the framework of fatherhood to the alien monarch and dominion over his realm[21]—and, above all, forgiveness.[22] What one might want to explore is how this vision, as sophisticated as generous, comes to occupy its place in Genesis, but this is outside my topic. As for sophistication, to get a full picture, one would have to pay attention to quite a few easily neglected details, such as the notion of 'to be angry' over your own misdeed.[23] Nor shall I probe John's deviations from the model. One, at first sight surprising, is his far lesser emphasis on forgiveness. Joseph grants it before his brothers have time to request it, in the same breath as he reveals his identity; and when after his father's death they fear reprisals, acknowledge their culpability and ask his pardon, he weeps, impresses on them that he is a mere human, not God, and promises to care for them—all of them, not excluding Judah. The Johannine Judas is a devil, is lost.[24]

There are further contacts with the Joseph tradition, though not all equally certain. John tells us that Judas, once Satan had entered into him, 'went out' into the night, i.e.

18. See J. Jeremias, art. '*polloi*', in *Theologisches Wörterbuch zum Neuen Testament*, ed. G. Friedrich, 1957, 6:536ff.

19. Amos 5.15.   20. II Kings 19.31, Isaiah 37.32.

21. Genesis 41.40ff., 45.8.   22. Genesis 45.5ff., 50.15ff.

23. Genesis 45.5. Where does it occur the first time elsewhere?

24. John 6.70, 17.12.

ceased to belong.[25] Some Rabbis go as far in their denunciation of Judah's crime as to see in the opening of the next chapter, 'And Judah went down from his brothers',[26] an indication of his expulsion.[27] My remark as to the self-censorship of our sources naturally applies with special force to such drastic interpretations: they would have wider currency two thousand years ago. Again, the city where Jesus meets the Samaritan woman is 'near the ground that Jacob gave Joseph'.[28] Conceivably an alert, near the outset, to Jesus taking up Joseph's repudiation of narrowly fixed boundaries.[29] It can be shown, I think, that the young Jesus's rejoinder in Luke that rather than cleave to his parents he must heed the concerns of his heavenly father connects up with Joseph's forgetting—being made to forget by God—his earthly father's house to fulfil his mission abroad.[30] Some repetitive phrasing in the lesson appended to the meeting may be significant: 'My meat is to do the will of him that sent me to finish his work', 'The works that my father has given me to finish bear witness that the father has sent me'—to which we should add a line from near the end: 'I have finished the work that you gave me to do'.[31]

Fresh light surely falls on Jesus's warning in John as he takes action against desecration of the Temple: 'Make not my father's house a house of trade'.[32] Note both 'my father's

25. John 13.30.

26. Genesis 38.1.

27. Genesis Rabba 85 on 38.1, Exodus Rabba 42 on 32.7, cited above, footnote 3. This possible ingredient in John's depiction I did ponder in *New Testament and Judaism*; cf. footnote 1.

28. John 4.5.

29. This is not to rule out the impact of a general association of Samaritans and Josephites.

30. Genesis 41.51, Luke 2.49; see above, footnote 7.

31. John 4.34, 5.36, 17.4.

32. John 2.16.

house', used by Joseph, and 'house of trade', recalling the
foreigners to whom he was sold and who are described as
'traders'.[33] The lower elements, we are given to understand,
are back—or still—at their plots, about to do to the new
Joseph what was done to the old. In this pericope, he acts
prophetically, programmatically, at the start of his mission.[34] His farewell discourse resumes the typology. 'In my
father's house are many mansions'[35] brings out the ample-
ness marking the house of Joseph's supreme father. (Side by
side with numerous further references. One of them is to
a yet earlier foretaste in the patriarchal cycle, the young
Rebekah's welcome of a stranger who has just entered the
town with his camels; she does not yet know that he is
Abraham's servant. He asks 'Is there room in your father's
house for us to lodge in?', to which she replies 'We have
both straw and provender enough and room to lodge in'.[36])
The sequel speaks of Jesus leaving in order to prepare a
place for those around him so that, after reunion, he may
fulfil all their desires: the Joseph pattern. Actually, they
ought to rejoice at his departure destined to lead to the
highest blessings for him and them: just as God turned evil
into good in the prefiguration. These gifts are bestowed by
the Father, in answer to Jesus's wishes: so behind Joseph
stood Pharaoh, occupying the throne.[37]

Even such advanced theological propositions as that
their future life in glory is assured by his own, or that they

33. Genesis 37.28.

34. See my 'Some Reflections on the Historicity of the New
Testament', *Catholic Commission on Intellectual and Cultural Affairs
Annual* 1986, pp. 3f.

35. John 14.2.

36. Genesis 24.23ff., cited at John 14.2 by D. Eb. Nestle,
Novum Testamentum Graece, 22d ed. by D. Er. Nestle and D. K.
Aland, 1956, p. 276.

37. Genesis 41.40ff., 45.8ff., 16ff.

should believe and see the Father in him, if for no other reason in view of his works, belong here. We must bear in mind that, in a sense, Joseph too died and rose. Quite apart from the general affinity between enslavement-liberation and death-rebirth, to Jacob at least it would totally feel that way. He was presented with proof that he whom 'he loved more than all his children'[38] had been torn to pieces by a wild beast; and he gave himself up to utter despair. 'He refused to be comforted . . . I will go down into the grave unto my son mourning'.[39] Josephus indeed depicts him as mourning 'like an only son's father'.[40] When, years later, his other sons told him that 'Joseph lives and is ruler throughout the land of Egypt',[41] he would not listen and—if we interpret in 'fundamentalist' fashion—well-nigh died himself really from such lack of faith: 'His heart grew cold for he believed them not'. They kept filling him in with details, however, and showed him the carriages Joseph had sent him for his journey—he saw Joseph's works, we might say—so he revived: 'His spirit lived'. The briefest mention may be made of a verbal point from pursuance of which in earnest we might never return: while Jacob would not be comforted till, after a long time, his spirit lived on taking in the glad tidings, John in this chapter has Jesus promise a Comforter, the spirit of truth, the holy spirit, that will help in difficult periods.[42]

Luckily, it is demonstrable that, for some at any rate of the first-century exegetes, Jacob's initial disbelief consti-

38. Genesis 37.3.

39. Genesis 37.35.

40. *Jewish Antiquities* 2.3.4.38. If the dead is not an only son, or if he can be replaced, a parent will be comforted: II Samuel 12.24, Job 42.11.

41. Genesis 45.26ff.

42. 14.16f., 26.

tuted a serious lapse; demonstrable from Josephus's strenu-
ous, direct contradiction of Scripture in this matter.[43] Already the Book of Jubilees seems to have felt it necessary to
exculpate the patriarch, ascribing his response to a black-
out;[44] and the Jerusalemite Targum and Pirqe de R. Eliezer
38 suppress the datum. Josephus's picture is extreme. Of
the wonderful reports, he writes, Jacob 'deemed none un-
believable, taking into consideration[45] God's power to perform great works[46] and his benevolence towards him even if
it was in abeyance for an interval'. What deserves particular
attention is that Jacob's attitude strikingly accords with that
prescribed for the disciples in John. Such is the resem-
blance, in fact, that one might suspect an old Christian in-
terpolation. It is unlikely, in my view. Note, however, that
even on that basis the passage would afford strong evidence
in favour of the part the Fourth Gospel, I maintain, assigns
to the Joseph drama—the interpolator representing a genuine tradition.

To conclude this section with what at the moment is just
an impression: the epic from Genesis, as understood by
later generations, may have contributed to facets of atonement in the New Testament. Jubilees, of the second century
B.C., makes it dominant in this department of religion: the
deed of the brothers took place on the tenth of the seventh
month, and that is why the Day of Atonement was ordained for this date. What is more, the offence against the

43. *Jewish Antiquities* 2.7.1.186f. See H. St. J. Thackeray, *Josephus* (Loeb Classical Library, 1930), 4:237 note a.
44. 43.24. An interest in excuses of this type comes out also in
41.25, stressing Judah's ignorance of Tamar's identity when he had
intercourse with her.
45. *Logizomai*, as in Caiaphas's reproach 'You do not consider';
see above, with footnote 9.
46. *Megalourgia*.

father is the most terrible element of the crime. The news that his son had perished made him weep on the tenth of the seventh month, the yearly atonement commemorates 'their grieving the affection of their father regarding Joseph his son'.[47] The Dead Sea sect read Jubilees and so, surely, did other fringe movements. Indeed, *non constat* that similar constructions were not once more widespread than it looks from our expurgated Rabbinic material.

V

Here are five headings which do fall under my subject and I feel bad sidetracking them.

1. Nature of the rulings and sanctions. To quote myself: 'We are moving in an uncomfortably ill-defined region where law, morality, politics and practical wisdom combine into a strange mixture'. In Hebrew, the forms mostly employed for these directions are ambiguous, translatable by 'must', 'should' or 'may', and if negative by 'must not', 'should not' or 'need not'. I quote myself again: 'Usually, in legal writings, the context enables us to pick the right nuance. In the province here under consideration, however, owing to its peculiar, indeterminate description, such help is greatly attenuated and a good deal remains nebulous'.[1] Take an advice that in such and such circumstances, 'they surrender a person'. Does this signify 'must surrender', 'should surrender', 'may surrender'? Interpretation will vary—and, up to a point, is meant to vary by the authors—according to period, general conditions, individual

47. 34.12ff. Translation by R. H. Charles, ed. *The Apocrypha and Pseudepigrapha of the Old Testament*, 1913, 2:65.

1. *Collaboration with Tyranny*, pp. 93, 95.

philosophy. A mess, more durable than order. In the so-called Haustafeln of the Epistles, incidentally, one of these forms is detectable behind the faulty Greek.[2] I would say that, on the whole, the obligations laid down there belong to the relatively stable category. A directive for slaves in I Peter, for example, doubtless means 'should': 'The slaves should subject themselves to their masters'.[3] 'May' would be inappropriate.

There are few strict sanctions in the ancient sources for unjustified surrender and none for unjustified non-surrender. Extra-legal punishment is a different matter. Judas found himself an outcast. He sought expiation in suicide in one version, suffered a violent death at the hand of heaven in another.[4] Simeon ben Johai, having returned to civilized life after years in hiding, recognized the disciple through whom the Romans had obtained their information. He looked at him and he turned into a heap of bones.[5] Whether modern attempts to bring such cases before the courts are a success, who can say?

2. The attitude of the victim. Calling for a study in depth. Isaac and Isaiah's Servant of the Lord are resigned and trusting. The former, it is true, starts out naively unaware,[6] but he must have known soon enough. Joseph resembles them in meekness. Frightened and begging for mercy as his ordeal is about to begin,[7] he ends up accepting it thankfully. Sheba surely fought to the end. Ullah acquiesced in his extradition, under gigantic pressure: besides the ultimatum as such, there were the representations of a host who up to then had protected him at heavy risk to himself. It is to Joshua ben Levi's credit that, called a betrayer by Elijah, he

2. See my *Ancient Jewish Law*, 1981, pp. 83f.
3. I Peter 2.18.   4. Matthew 27.3ff., Acts 1.18ff.
5. Babylonian Shabbath 34b.   6. Genesis 22.7f.
7. Genesis 42.21.

did not plead Ullah's consent in excuse. Among Greek play-wrights, Euripides is a veritable specialist in the shades of willingness to lay down one's life for others.[8] His Macaria prefers to be slaughtered straightaway to being chosen for slaughter by lot: the latter may be more just but is less gracious.[9] (In the twelve years or so of involvement in medi-cal ethics, I became very aware of the complexity of 'vol-untarism', say, in donating a kidney to your brother or subjecting yourself to a dangerous experiment.)[10] An ex-tremely intricate case which would have to figure is Jonah:[11] as the boat on which he was fleeing from God was about to sink in a tempest, he got the company to rescue themselves by throwing him overboard—the same man who, little later, resents the reprieve of Nineveh. I shall still have to say a word about another aspect of this near-disaster at sea.

Jesus offers himself up wholeheartedly. Yet, at Geth-semane, he does pray for the cup to pass from him—except in the Fourth Gospel, where his readiness is absolute.[12] It displays the same tendency elsewhere. Thus, Jesus cooper-ates with Judas to a striking extent.[13] Partly this may be due to the latter being a devil—as I mentioned before—less

8. See J. Schmitt, 'Freiwilliger Opfertod bei Euripides', in *Religionsgeschichtliche Versuche und Vorarbeiten*, ed. L. Deubner, L. Malten and O. Weinreich, 1921, vol. 17, pt. 2.

9. Euripides, *The Children of Hercules* 543ff.

10. See e.g. my 'Transplantation: Acceptability of Procedures and the Required Legal Sanctions', in *Ciba Foundation Symposium on Ethics in Medical Progress*, ed. G. E. W. Wolstenholme and M. O'Connor, 1966, pp. 197f.; and 'Legal Problems in Medical Ad-vance', The Hebrew University of Jerusalem Lionel Cohen Lec-ture 16, 1971, pp. 8ff., rept. *Israel Law Review* 6 (1971): 4ff.

11. See my 'Jonah: A Reminiscence', *Journal of Jewish Studies* 35 (1984): 36ff.

12. Matthew 26.39, Mark 14.36, Luke 22.42.

13. E.g. John 18.2; see Bauer, *Johannesevangelium*, p. 203.

than human, a mere instrument for a purpose. But it also serves to underline the single-mindedness of the former. As for Gethsemane, John virtually criticizes the other tradition when he puts a rhetorical question into Jesus's mouth: 'The cup which my Father has given me, shall I not drink it?'[14] It is uttered, by the way, to stop Peter's armed attack on the band come for his arrest. The incident, therefore, takes the place (of course, this is only a fraction of what it does) of one recorded in Matthew and Mark—and omitted by Luke—where Peter will not tolerate Jesus's fateful predictions, no doubt hoping for, if need be, a victorious battle, and is rebuffed: 'Away from me, Satan, you intend not the things of God but those of men'.[15] This connection is verified by the fact that it is only John who identifies the violent disciple as Peter; in all three Synoptics he is anonymous.

In the appendix of the Fourth Gospel, Jesus foresees the crucifixion of Peter, by then grown old and feeble in body. What deserves notice here is the phrasing of his emotions as that ordeal occurs: he will be carried 'whither he would not want [to go]'.[16] Human nature does assert itself—even in a genuine martyr.

A last point. In Matthew and Mark, as Jesus is taken, the disciples escape. Luke omits this detail. In John, they have no need to flee: Jesus requests the officers, since it is he whom they consider a threat, not to touch the rest.[17] This version is widely assumed to aim at exonerating his companions.[18] It is certainly one aim. But another, more conformable to the text—'of them whom you gave me I have

14. John 18.11, cf. 12.27.
15. Matthew 16.23, Mark 8.33, cf. Luke 9.22ff.
16. John 21.18.
17. Matthew 26.56, Mark 14.50, John 18.8f.
18. See Bauer, *Johannesevangelium*, p. 204.

lost none'—is to have Jesus do for his proximate circle the same as for the world at large.[19] He will sacrifice himself for the former no less than for the latter. Once more, a faint echo of the Joseph epic may be perceptible.

3. Bystanders. (Would be a good title for a reflective essay, taking in all varieties; for instance, that extreme character, the bystander to whatever befalls himself.) Two summary pronouncements in the New Testament are clearly relevant though going far beyond the specific situation of this lecture: 'He that is not against us is for us' (originally, Caesar's mode of assessment—secure, noble) and 'He that is not with me is against me' (originally, the mode Caesar attributed to his opponents—insisting on visible adherence to the party line).[20] In our day, Hochhuth, his supporters and his critics are among those who have wrestled with the problem of passivity in dilemmas not unlike that here examined.

4. The line-up. Owing to the vagueness of the dicta, it is not too clear even what constitutes a collective for their purposes and what an outside foe. Caiaphas manoeuvred in defence of the nation, precariously holding up under its

19. See C. K. Barrett, *The Gospel According to St. John*, 1955, pp. 431, 435.

20. Matthew 12.30, Mark 9.40, Luke 9.50, 11.23, Cicero, *Pro Ligario* 11.35. In connection with Luke 9.50, H. L. Strack and P. Billerbeck, *Kommentar zum Neuen Testament aus Talmud und Midrasch*, 4 vols., 1924–1929, rept. 1969, 2:165, adduce Jose ben Bun, fourth century, who sees in Psalms 1.1, 'Blessed is the man that walks not in the counsels of the ungodly', the merciful assurance that shunning these counsels equals following those of the just. No doubt there are points of affinity but, on the whole, the setting and focus of the quote make it rather distant from the Caesar-generated proverb. On the Talmudic background, see C. G. Montefiore and H. Loewe, *A Rabbinic Anthology*, 1938, rept. with prolegomenon by R. Loewe, 1974, pp. 595f.

Roman overlord. According to John, we saw, Jesus surrendered himself also for the more intimate body formed by
his disciples. Joshua ben Levi feared for the congregation of
Lydda. Whether Ullah actually belonged to it, however,
and indeed whether this datum mattered, we cannot say.[21]
Right at the beginning, you may remember, I catalogued a
quite different, cruder case, a party of travellers given the
choice by heathen brigands between handing over one and
being murdered all. One common characteristic which
does stand out is the vastly superior strength of the ha-
rasser. Without exception, the various solutions to the
ghastly problem I have inspected were tried out by the Jews
in the fixed role of underdogs.

Obviously, even of two more or less equal groups, one
may threaten the other with dire consequences unless it de-
livers up somebody at discretion. My speaking of 'more or
less equal' is an admission that the situation is not rigidly
separable from my principal interest. Still, the Book of
Judges offers a good enough illustration.[22] An abominable
deed was committed against a Levite visitor in a Benja-
minite city. The other tribes gave Benjamin an opportunity
to extradite the perpetrators. It was scorned and after pro-
longed, ruinous fighting Benjamin was defeated. It would
indeed have ceased to exist had the victors not taken special
measures towards its recovery—a fraternal posture which,
as observed above,[23] the Jews did not expect ever of their

21. For Josephus, *Jewish Antiquities* 7.11.8.291, a consideration
making it easier for the inhabitants of Sheba's last stronghold to
throw him to the wolves was that he was an unknown: the Biblical
text contains nothing to this effect. See my 'Nuances of Exposition in Luke-Acts', in *Aufstieg und Niedergang der römischen Welt*,
pt. 2, Principat, vol. 25, ed. W. Haase, 1985, p. 2350.

22. 19ff.

23. Under II, towards the end.

masters. There is an entire genre of Greek plays about sanctuary to a fugitive from abroad in the face of his country's remonstrations. In the oldest one preserved, the *Suppliant Maidens* by Aeschylus, Argos grants the Danaides asylum though their Egyptian pursuers, claiming them as their brides, have given notice that this will mean war.[24]

Again, nowadays, over a large part of the globe, if a man kills or robs, the public organs are charged with his punishment and his family is supposed to abide by the verdict. In many an ancient society, it was a matter between the two families.[25] Change set in as, more and more frequently, the injured family would gain the cooperation of others. Even at this stage, not seldom the two sides might be fairly balanced, and it took time—and inducements of all sorts—for the abandonment of the malefactor to become automatic. As is well known, there are pockets of the previous system left in states with the most up-to-date judicial institutions.

For a really thorough evaluation of the Rabbinic canons, all these adjoining fields would have to be taken into account.

5. Theocracy. Somewhat akin to the Jewish wayfarers set upon by savages is the community in the Book of Jonah, and a truer stand on humanity it is difficult to imagine. The crew of the vessel were gentiles, yet far from religious harmony: in the storm, 'every man cried to his god'. Certainly nothing tied them to the person of Jonah who, immediately on being admitted, withdrew to sleep in a corner and only appeared when the captain woke him so he might implore his god too. The lots proved him to be the stirrer-up of

24. See B. Daube, *Rechtsprobleme im Agamemnon*, pp. 74ff.
25. Plenty of literature. I have tackled some questions in *Studies in Biblical Law*, 1947, rept. 1969, pp. 213ff., and *The Defence of Superior Orders in Roman Law*, 1956, pp. 19f., rept. *Law Quarterly Review* 72 (1956): 501f.

heaven's wrath. Now he introduced himself and exhorted them to hurl him into the waves, thus ensuring their safety. But so strong was their dedication to the bond between any aboard their ship that, notwithstanding the danger, they laboured long and hard before they could bring themselves to take this step. (I commute from San Francisco to Berkeley by the first bus about half past five in the morning. There is definitely a degree of comradery between the regulars—and of hostility to the occasional intruder—but I assure you that we do not come up to the standard of those pagan seadogs.) In terms of this discussion, here was a summons, on pain of universal extinction, to extradite a specific individual guilty, as he himself acknowledged, of the crassest dereliction of duty—and these 'Noachides' felt like resisting.

Perhaps the most arresting feature of the embroglio is that the oppressor making the hateful demand was God. By rights, it should not need to be pointed out at all seeing that a large proportion of human sacrifices from inside a collective everywhere are designed to gratify a deity otherwise at odds with it, and often, indeed, the deity wants not a designated individual like Jonah but simply one or more victims no matter who they are—what the Rabbis would not submit to even in an epoch of terror. Thus, at one time, if Rome was in peril, anything born that spring, animal or human, was forfeit to Jupiter.[26] The Theban general Pelopidas, bidden in a dream on the eve of battle to slaughter a virgin—any virgin so long as she had auburn hair—refused.[27] When Korah and other grandees rose against Moses and Aaron, the bulk of the people were ordered to distance themselves from them if they did not wish to share their

---

26. Festus, *De Significatu Verborum*, Pauli Excerpta 379. Far be it from me to pronounce on the question of historicity.

27. Plutarch, *Parallel Lives*, Pelopidas 21.1.

fate.[28] Those condemned were manifestly guilty, not just an undefined crowd—though their innocent households, let us not overlook, were wiped out with them.[29] In this case it was God himself who executed the sentence; as they had challenged the leadership, it was essential for the answer to come from one standing above both parties. Achan, who appropriated sacred booty from Jericho, was put to death—together with his innocent household—by the community.[30] The latter, to begin with, had been unaware of his offence. But the army got into desperate straits. God informed Joshua that an impious theft was the cause, indicated a method by which to identify the culprit and declared that, unless he was burnt, the people would be rendered no more help. Arguably, in a theocracy, any capital punishment includes an element—from strong to faint—of duress from on high: the villain is offered up lest, if he is not, the community be doomed. Naturally, this is most conspicuous where a crime affects the deity directly, idolatry, for example. But it is traceable elsewhere too: 'If a man hates his neighbour and smites him that he dies, your eye shall not pity him but you shall put away the blood of the innocent from Israel, that it may go well with you'.[31]

A thorough comparison of extradition to terrestrial potentates and extradition to supernatural ones would greatly further our understanding of both. Roughly, the latter started by being modelled on the former, but then developed its own momentum and, while constantly receiving fresh impulses from below, in turn exercised strong influence. Just as, say, the picture of God as judge took off from the this-worldly institution, then sprouted more and more traits of its own, and time came when the judge above would be held out for imitation to the original. Similarly, at

28. Numbers 16.26.   29. Mitigated in Numbers 26.11.
30. Joshua 7.   31. Deuteronomy 19.11ff.

first, 'the exodus was construed as an application, on a higher plane, of social usages familiar from the daily world; once the story in this form had gained currency, however, it in its turn had an enormous impact on social affairs'.[32] Some proto-Pharisaic principle of defending to the last a fellow-member of your caravan from human raiders, whatever their motivation, must have been held in profound respect when the sailors of the first chapter of Jonah attempted to enforce it against the Almighty tracking down a deserter.

The extent of overlap may be gauged from narratives where it is scarcely possible to say whether a community confronts an earthly claimant or a higher one. Minos waged war against Attica, supported by the gods who sent pestilence and barrenness. It was the gods, too, who told the Athenians to accept his terms: a tribute every few years of a number of youngsters to be devoured by the Minotaur.[33] Were they delivered up to the gods or to the foreign adversary? In David's reign there was a famine and the Lord informed him of the cause, a wrong done the Gibeonites by Saul.[34] Asked what amends they desired, they replied that they wanted seven of Saul's sons whom they would hang up to the Lord—which was done. Extradition to the Gibeonites or to the Lord?[35] I shall not proceed with this.

(Here is a warning should anyone do so. I have confined myself to the area of human sacrifice closest to the central conundrum of this lecture, i.e. where a collective, not to

32. See my *The Exodus Pattern in the Bible*, 1963, p. 16.
33. Plutarch, *Parallel Lives*, Theseus 15.1.
34. II Samuel 21.
35. As well as, in part, to David himself, so to speak, who would welcome their demise. The sacrificer's interest, crudely apparent in this case, will on scrutiny turn out not to be totally absent in quite a few others.

succumb, has to cede one or more of its members to the gods. From this, we must mark off the case where a person in power, not to succumb, has to cede a human possession—a father his son or daughter, a husband his wife, a monarch one or more of his subjects. Jephtha promised the Lord whoever of his household would welcome him first on his victorious return—happened to be his only child.[36] Artemis, offended by Agamemnon, produced a calm so the Greek fleet under his command could not sail against Troy; whereupon he donated to her his daughter Iphigeneia. Though the two situations—a community abandoning a member, a person in power abandoning a subordinate— share obvious similarities, there are also huge political and moral differences and their histories are far from smoothly parallel. By and large, we have before us the distinction between communal responsibility and ruler punishment I advocated for ancient jurisprudence long ago.[37] I noted then that intermediate and mixed varieties abound. Insofar as Jesus was betrayed in order to placate the Romans, his was the very type of extradition controversial between Pharisees and Sadducees. When the First Epistle of John has him sent by his father for a propitiation,[38] he becomes more like Isaac whom Abraham, his father, the person in power, is willing to slay on mount Moriah. Needless to say, as the father in I John is God himself, this is not all.)

A final aside about the Book of Jonah. That God seem-

---

36. Judges 11.30ff. Rabbinic exegesis, bent on mitigating his ruthlessness, makes him vow not 'whoever would first meet him' but 'whatever'—thinking of a goat or a dog: Josephus, *Jewish Antiquities* 5.7.10.263f., Genesis Rabba 60 on 24.13. See my 'Texts and Interpretation in Roman and Jewish Law', *Jewish Journal of Sociology* 3 (1961): 25.

37. See my *Studies in Biblical Law*, pp. 160ff.

38. 4.10.

ingly deals with the oarsmen like the grimmest tyrant is in keeping with the entire paradoxical constitution of the work. Its prophet tries to quit his service not because his master is cruel but because he is all-merciful: which makes it a fool's errand to preach that disaster will follow sin. He is forced back and does prove right again. Yet, as the curtain comes down, the wicked Ninevites have repented—for the moment at least—and he himself has learnt—for the moment at least—a lot about God's reasons. Just so, the mariners, having held out for brotherhood under severe testing, reach land and adore the Lord of creation—to the accompaniment, indeed, of a chant by Jonah in the whale's belly.[39] Everything is stood on its head, yet comes out profoundly alright.[40]

VI

In the late fifties and early sixties I talked on this complex to various audiences, and perhaps my most interesting lecture now would concern their various responses. My poor youngest son was around ten when I asked him what he would do as the mayor if bidden to supply two male citizens—any two—for a spectacular execution, otherwise all

39. Jonah 1.16, 'The men offered a sacrifice unto the Lord and made vows', 2.9, 'I will sacrifice unto you, I will pay what I vowed'; see 'Jonah: A Reminiscence', p. 41.

40. Familiarity renders one insensitive to a further, momentous contradiction, not relevant to the subject in hand. We hear of a boat battling a gale, a passenger thrown into the sea and swallowed by a fish, a city utterly depraved—but, throughout, not one person is killed. The same is true of another masterpiece in praise of the misfit: in the whole of *Don Quixote*, including part 1 and part 2, a persiflage, after all, of the knightly exploits then popular, there is not a single killing.

males of the town would be shot; and, of course, he was not allowed to offer himself. He replied that he must assume to have been elected for the town's welfare, so he would accede—and then commit suicide. No wonder he has taken himself off to Western Australia, safe from his father. My experience in general was that the less familiar my listeners were with the realities of tyranny, the more unhesitating they were in saying No. Occasionally, when meeting with a lively, informal undergraduate group, I took a vote: who would appease and who would resist? And felt real admiration for the handful with the courage of coming out for compliance.

American academics inclined to be overreliant on unilinear logic. At a law seminar, a number of colleagues took it for granted that the Strasbourg dilemma would remain the same if the Commandant, instead of conducting a *razzia*, had told the parents to bring one boy to be shot or else he would seize both: ergo a mother of the sort Helen had in mind would grab one and take him to headquarters. Utterly mistaken. No doubt she would thereby be avoiding a double loss. But this does not erase the huge difference of the scenario as a whole, involving—among other things—a brutal act. My hunch is that a mother would be almost less capable of it than a father.

A frequent Marxist approach in East Germany and Russia was to deny any special problem: you simply, as in every situation, take the course most helpful for continuing the war against the class enemy. The Strasbourg father should have saved a son: one more fighter on the right side. Looks superficially like Helen's impulse but is, at bottom, miles apart. In most cases—for example, that just posited: bring us one child in order to keep the other—even the outer results would be different. (I shall be content with hinting at a distinct, highly important aspect: the inadequacy, even within a thoroughly materialistic philosophy, of a mechanical head–count for assessing gain and loss. One could imagine that the shooting of the two brothers, by creating widespread abhorrence, did the occupying power more harm than it would have suffered at the hands of a survivor.) I did, however, hear other views even behind the iron curtain: Marxism is not one rigidly unitary system. Also, now and then, I got one answer from officials in the open debate and another from humbler folks afterwards, in conversation.

As I am putting the finishing touches to this paper, my friend Walter Weyrauch sends me a pioneering study of betrayal.[1] While dealing in depth with Gestapo informants[2]— the inducements, likely and unlikely candidates, their fate—he sketches a comprehensive theory of undercover operations, with glimpses at confidential information in answer to job or credit inquiries and, indeed, at any scholar's pursuit of truth qua gathering of hitherto secret data for 'intelligence' purposes. Which puts me in mind of the sixties, when John (now Lord) Butterworth, Vice-Chancellor of Warwick University, got into trouble with the students: they found out that he had scribbled on a youngster's application file which he passed on to the admission committee, 'Was co–editor of a radical school–magazine'. I was told of

1. 'Gestapo Informants: Facts and Theory of Undercover Operations', *Columbia Journal of Transnational Law* 24 (1986): 553ff.

2. Incidentally, the account—see above, under III, footnote 1—of how the Romans got to know about Simeon ben Johai's attacks shows that they had informants telling them not only of enemies but also of friends and neutrals: Judah ben Ilai is mentioned as on their side. It very much looks as if the Rabbi's disciple had in fact been such a general informant, though just conceivably he was but a careless talker—maybe among his gentile relations— and someone else made the damaging report.

this by Alan (now Lord) Bullock at Oxford who, a far more experienced hand at university government, added: 'He doesn't seem to know what the telephone is for'.[3]

Occasionally the question is raised why Jewish suffering attracts more than average attention. I visited Cambodia before the Vietnamese war and fell in love with that civilisation—and I mean the whole civilisation, not just the famous sculptures. It is gone for ever, destroyed by invaders who had as little awareness as an ox that tramples over the black tulip. A holocaust; but, honestly, are there many who care? One factor, however minor, may be precisely what is exemplified by the material before us: a continuous, conscious turning over of the agonies throughout the millennia among those afflicted and within each of them, a never-ending re-experience, modified yet enhanced by changes in culture, often refined, at times debased, always rich far beyond the temporary, and—springing from it at once and fostering it—an attempt to draw lessons and provide signposts, tentative though they must be, for succeeding generations plunged into the same gruelling impasse. You cannot be in touch with this mood without feeling that not one sparrow is forgotten before God.[4]

3. Anticipating Nixon's 'Destroy all tapes'. The comment has more point in England than in the States, on two grounds. First, even yet, over there, the note has not lost out to the call, so it takes a clever guy to discover where the latter has advantages; and second, even yet, over there, bugging is not commonplace.

4. Matthew 10.29, Luke 12.6. According to Jerusalemite Shebiith 38d, cited by Strack and Billerbeck, *Kommentar*, 1:582, Simeon ben Johai, when after thirteen years in a cave he had an inkling that conditions had improved, reached his decision to return by observing a man catching birds with a net. Each time a heavenly voice proclaimed salvation, the little creature escaped; and he concluded that since no bird could perish against the Lord's

will, surely no human could. How touching that, in this quandary, he made use of the established logic of the a fortiori. —On rereading, I cannot leave it at that. Babylonian Shabbath 33b is simpler and, I guess, later: no birds, and a heavenly voice just counsels the fugitive to go forth from his cave. His contact with the above is manifestly no less intimate in the Jerusalemite version, so why the complication, the indirectness? Because God here behaves like a great teacher with a gifted pupil, supplying a signal but leaving room for interpretation and choice of action. All over the world, wisdom instruction—especially if of an esoteric flavour—cultivates this method. As for Simeon's prowess in the art of inference, I have argued that he learnt from Labeo's *ratio* and *regula* ('Jewish Law in the Hellenistic World', *Jewish Law Annual*, suppl. 2, 1980, pp. 58ff.). With the particular deduction in this case, cf., for example, his gloss on Isaiah 65.22, 'As the days of a tree are the days of my people': the tree is the Torah and since the Torah, created in honour of Israel, will endure throughout this and the next worlds, all the more will the pious ones for whose sake the world was created (Siphre Deuteronomy 47 on 11.21, see W. Bacher, *Die Agada der Tannaiten*, 1890, rept. 1966, 2:146). —Clearly, this final footnote is destined to link up with the beginning. When I rhapsodized to Helen about that reticent, oblique kind of guidance, she remarked that men taught thus but not women; the latter came right out. This seems accurate. I suppose it is explicable by women, so far at least, having their vital teaching experience with infants, where you must be to the point: 'Don't touch the hot iron'. Men take over at a stage when the abler ones among their charges ought to be steered towards independence.

Appendix
Jesus among the Sages

As is well known, the Lukan tale of the young Jesus among the teachers in the Temple[1] calls to mind numerous cases of future greatness manifested in boyhood. J. M. Creed[2] singles out Cyrus who quite early showed his royal qualities at play,[3] Alexander who was not much older when making an impression on ambassadors he received in his father's absence,[4] Apollonius who at age fourteen surpassed his tutors in wisdom and application[5] and Josephus who in his autobiography relates[6] that he was consulted at that age on points of law by high priests and other notables. Without disputing the relevance of these pieces, I think there is another which has directly contributed to the shaping of the story, namely, the dreams of Joseph, aged seventeen years, in Genesis.[7]

For my purpose it is enough to quote the second one which he reports to his father as well as his brothers. In it, sun, moon and eleven stars prostrate themselves before him. His father rebukes him for his arrogance, at the same time storing the incident in his memory. In Luke, as Jesus's parents leave Jerusalem with their caravan, he, without informing them, stays behind to debate in the Temple. After a day's journey they notice his absence, return and are struck with amazement on finally locating him in the midst of an admiring audience. His mother reproaches him for his un-

---

1. 2.41ff.; see above, under IV, with footnotes 7 and 30.
2. *The Gospel According to St. Luke*, 1930, p. 44.
3. Herodotus, *Histories* 1.114ff.
4. Plutarch, *Parallel Lives*, Alexander 5.1.
5. Philostratus, *Life of Apollonius* 1.7.
6. *Life* 2.9.
7. 37.5ff.

filial behaviour but he majestically overrides her complaint. The parents do not understand, yet his mother keeps everything in her heart.

That there are weighty differences is obvious. To name a few—Joseph is less far along his road than Jesus. Thus, whereas the former's break with the norm consists in a vision and his promulgation of it, the latter's consists in actions; and whereas the former does not refute the censure meted out to him, the latter does. Again, the dominant role of Joseph's father contrasts with that of Jesus's mother. This is just one illustration of a general datum: the father's attachment is to the fore throughout Joseph's life, the mother's throughout Jesus's. (I am speaking of earthly parents.) Still, the similarities are too striking to be due to chance. Apart from the main theme, i.e. an omen from heaven of glory to come, in both pericopes the hero commits an apparent wrong, upsets traditional authority within the family, assumes a status not yet recognizably his. In both one parent pleads with him and in both in the name of the other parent too: Jacob exclaims 'Shall I and your mother and your brothers bow down ourselves?', Mary 'Why have you thus dealt with us? Your father and I have sought you'. In both, the leading parent, while on one level offended and while far from thorough comprehension, does sense another dimension and will go on pondering the matter. The phraseology is much the same: the LXX writes *ho de pater autou dieterese to rema*, the evangelist *kai he meter autou dieterei panta ta remata en kardia autes*.[8]

---

8. Naturally, subsequent re-interpretation, too, presents similarities. According to Josephus, Jacob, far from protesting, expresses delight (*Jewish Antiquities* 2.3.3.15). J.-P. Migne explains (ed. *Scriptura Sacra*, vol. 22, 1862, col. 463) that Mary's 'Why have you thus dealt with us?' *interrogatio est, non reprehensionis, accusationis aut querimoniae, sed admirationis.*

With regard to phraseology, there is a further detail of interest. Jesus asserts that he must be 'in what are my father's', *en tois tou patros mou*. Creed, representing the prevalent opinion, rightly gives it the sense 'in my father's home'—on the basis of Septuagintal usage. Joseph, we learn in Genesis,[9] calls his firstborn Manasseh, *Menashshe* in Hebrew, 'for God has made me forget, *nashshani*, all my toil and all my father's house'; the Septuagint renders the concluding words 'all that are my father's', *panton ton tou patros mou*. My point is that we have before us not a mere linguistic coincidence, but a harking back of the New Testament narrative to the Old Testament one. The latter brings out a moment when Joseph becomes so filled by his marvellous present as to no longer have a stake in the past. Something of this kind happens to the young Jesus at the Temple. Only Joseph by 'my father's home' designates his old world now, under God's direction, left behind, Jesus his new world now totally claiming him—'my true father's home', we might expand. In passing—Mary's address 'child', *teknon*, has a remarkable counterpart in Reuven's lament on finding Joseph gone from the pit:[10] 'The child is not', with *yeledh* referring to a seventeen-year-old lad. The Septuagint does justice to the Hebrew though, to be sure, by means of *paidarion*, not *teknon*.

Thirty years ago I wondered[11] whether New Testament writers connected Jesus's treacherous disciple with that brother of Joseph who devised his sale, both bearing the name Judah or Judas; and I said probably not, and indeed that Joseph appeared nowhere to be treated as prefiguring Jesus. By now I am certain that I was wrong on both counts. John's Caiaphas, for instance, in his prophecy about Jesus's

9. 41.51.
10. Genesis 37.50.
11. See my *New Testament and Rabbinic Judaism*, pp. 3f.

death, can be shown to allude to Joseph's saving mission to the Egyptians threatened by famine.[12] I am setting out the documentation in the preceding lecture; and am content here to point out that the episode under review evidently contains hints allied to those in the Fourth Gospel.

No doubt the bulk of the occurrence is pre-Lukan. The easy tone of the discourse with the Sages, highlighted by its elimination from the Infancy Gospel of Thomas, mid-second century,[13] speaks for an early date. Moreover, had he been formulating on his own, he would hardly have depicted the parents as forgetful of the previous predictions by the shepherds, Simeon and Anna.[14] Lastly, I have suggested[15] that the final reference to Jesus's subjection[16] is appended to the nucleus which had a tripartite structure familiar from many encounters: revolutionary action—protest—silencing of the remonstrants. By Luke's time, with a fair number of homes already fully Christian, Messianic zeal must be tempered with respect for worthy progenitors. Nevertheless, though he is not its author, his choice of the story does prove him to be in sympathy with it. Perhaps, to the considerations met in the literature, we may now add its universalist tendency, its linking Jesus's first public statement—uttered in the holiest of places—with Joseph's work for gentiles, in fact, gentiles who would soon oppress his people. J. Massyngberde Ford[17] has recently argued a sharp division between the infancy legends,

12. John 11.52, Genesis 45.5ff., 50.20, Psalms 105.17.

13. 19.2.

14. Luke 2.15ff.; see Creed, *Gospel According to Luke*, pp. 44, 46.

15. See my *Civil Disobedience in Antiquity*, pp. 47ff.

16. Luke 2.51.

17. See *My Enemy Is My Guest*, 1984. Yes, her initial stands for Josephine.

reflecting traditional, nationalistic expectations, and the main Third Gospel. Simeon and Anna, she proposes,[18] 'may have been anticipating a political leader'. Thereafter, however, 'Luke will . . . show that Jesus . . . is a preacher with . . . the powerful message of . . . loving one's enemy in word and deed'. The foregoing remarks seem to fit in with her thesis.

18. See *My Enemy Is My Guest*, p. 35.

Index of
Passages Cited

I. Old Testament and Related Sources

Genesis

1.27 . . . . 17 ff.
2.24 . . . . 18 f.
5.2 . . . . 17 ff.
6.9 . . . . 27 ff., 66
7.9 19
9.25 2
9.26 2
12.11 ff. 36
17.1 67
20.2 ff. 36
22.7 f. 100
24.23 ff. 96
29.21 ff. 36
37.3 97
37.5 ff. . . . . 115 ff.
37.18 ff. 90
37.26 f. 90
37.28 96
37.35 97
37.50 117
38.1 95
41.40 ff. 94, 96
41.51 . . . . 95, 117

42.21 100
44.17 ff. 90
45.5 . . . . 92 ff.
45.5 ff. 89, 94, 118
45.8 . . . . 92, 94
45.8 ff. 96
45.16 ff. 96
45.26 ff. 97
50.15 ff. 94
50.20 . . . . 92, 118
50.20 f. 89

Exodus

3.6 . . . . 4 ff.
5.21 84
20.13 2
21.24 . . . . 19 ff.
29.33 42

Leviticus

6.16 45
24.9 45

Numbers

5.30 f. 30

Numbers (*continued*)

12.12 . . . . 70 ff.
16.26 107
17.11 66
20.7 ff. 73
21.16 ff. 73
26.11 107
28.9 f. 46

Deuteronomy

5.17 2
11.9 4
11.21 4
17.17 19
19.11 ff. 107
20.20 46
21.20 . . . . 24 ff.
22.6 f. 84
24.7 80
25.11 21
31.16 . . . . 5, 30

Joshua

7 107

Judges

11.30 ff. 109
15.9 ff. . . . . 79 f.
19 ff. 104

I Samuel

1.12 ff. 26
17.25 42
21.1 ff. 46
21.3 47

II Samuel

11 36
12.24 97
20 . . . . 82 f., 88
21 108

II Kings

4.42 32
19.31 94

Isaiah

6.3 13
26.19 7
37.32 94
45.7 17
50.6 23
65.22 114

Hosea

4.14 30
5.7 42

Amos

5.15 94

Jonah

1 . . . . 101, 105 f., 108
1.16 110
2.9 110

Psalms

1.1 103
17.15 32
105.17 ff. 91, 118

Proverbs

23.20 f. 24

Job

3.16 69
19.15 42
19.17 42
42.11 97

Ruth

2.12 66
2.14 . . . . 32 f.
3.4 34
3.9 . . . . 34 f.

Lamentations

3.30 23

Ecclesiastes

6.3 69

Daniel

12.2 9

Sirach

9.9 24
18.33 24
45.4 71
45.18 42

I Maccabees

2.39 ff. 46
7.6 ff. 87, 91

II Maccabees

14.3 ff. 87, 91

IV Maccabees

7.19 . . . . 6, 9
16.25 . . . . 6, 9

Jubilees

34.12 ff. . . . . 98 f.
41.25 98
43.24 98

Testament of Levi

14.6 62

Psalms of Solomon

16.4 68

II. New Testament and Related Sources

Matthew

1.18 ff. 35
5.38 . . . . 19 ff.
9.10 ff. 23, 40
10.4 90
10.16 50
10.29 113
11.19 . . . . 23 ff.
12.1 ff. 46
12.6 57
12.30 103
14.3 ff. 89
14.20 . . . . 32 f.
15.37 . . . . 32 f.
16.23 102
17.24 ff. . . . . 39 ff.
18.1 ff. 41
18.6 55
19.3 ff. 17 ff.
21.2 ff. 50
21.23 ff. 31

22.21 . . . . 51 ff.
22.29 . . . . 6 f.
22.31 f. 4 ff.
24.22 ff. 16
24.37 f. 28
26.14 ff. 90
26.18 f. 50
26.21 ff. 90
26.39 101
26.45 ff. 90
26.56 102
27.3 ff. 90, 100

Mark

2.15 ff. 23, 40
2.33 ff. 46
3.21 26
6.17 ff. 89
6.42 f. . . . . 32 f.
6.45 ff. 16
8.8 . . . . 32 f.
8.33 102

Mark (*continued*)

9.33 f. 41
9.40 103
9.42 55
10.2 ff. . . . . 17 ff.
11.2 ff. 50
11.16 48
11.27 ff. 31
12.13 ff. 52
12.17 . . . . 51 ff.
12.24 . . . . 6 ff.
12.26 f. . . . . 4 ff.
12.28 15
12.34 f. 40
14.10 f. 90
14.13 ff. 50
14.18 ff. 90
14.36 101
14.41 ff. 90
14.50 102

Luke

1.35 ff. . . . . 33 ff.
2.15 ff. 118
2.41 ff. . . . . 91, 115 ff.
2.49 95
2.51 118
3.19 f. 89
5.29 ff. 23, 40
6.1 ff. 46
6.29 19
7.34 . . . . 23 ff.
7.36 ff. 23
9.17 . . . . 32 f.
9.22 ff. 102
9.46 ff. 41
9.50 103
11.5 ff. 27
11.23 103
12.6 113
13.31 89
15.1 ff. 23

16.1 ff. . . . . 26 ff.
17.2 55
17.26 f. 28
18.1 ff. 27, 42
19.30 ff. 50
20.1 ff. 31
20.20 53
20.25 . . . . 51 ff.
20.37 f. . . . . 4 ff.
22.3 ff. 90
22.10 ff. 50
22.21 ff. 90
22.42 101
22.47 ff. 90
23.2 53
23.11 ff. 89
24.37 16
24.39 16

John

1.27 93
2.7 . . . . 32 f.
2.16 . . . . 95 f.
2.19 ff. 12
3.16 f. 92
4.5 95
4.17 ff. 41
4.34 . . . . 93, 95
5.36 95
6.11 ff. . . . . 32 f.
6.70 94
8.7 . . . . 29 ff.
10.12 ff. 89
11.48 86
11.50 86
11.51 f. 89
11.52 118
11.53 89
12.27 102
13.2 ff. 90
13.21 ff. 90
13.30 95

14.2 96
14.16 f. 97
14.26 97
16.7 89
17.4 95
17.12 94
18.2 101
18.2 ff. 90
18.8 f. 102
18.11 102
18.14 86
19.11 92
21.18 102

Acts

1.18 ff. 100
2.24 10
3.13 ff. 14
4.2 14
5.30 14
9.4 68
22.6 ff. 15
22.7 68
22.16 69
23.8 . . . . 14 f.
23.9 15
26.14 68

Romans

8 16
8.3 92
13.1 ff. 58
13.6 f. 53

I Corinthians

5.1 ff. 61
6.14 9
7.12 ff. . . . . 61 f.
10.4 73
15.6 9

15.8 . . . . 69 ff.
15.9 59
15.20 9
15.43 9
15.44 ff. 16
15.51 . . . . 9, 15

II Corinthians

13.4 9

Galatians

1.16 68
4.4 . . . . 92 f.

Philemon 62

I Peter

2.4 ff. 57
2.18 100

I John

4.9 . . . . 92 f.
4.10 . . . . 92 f., 109
4.14 . . . . 92 f.

Hebrews

3.2 71

Gospel according to the Hebrews

8 11

Infancy Gospel of Thomas

19.2 118

Athenagoras
Plea for the Christians 31.1 63

Eusebius
Ecclesiastical History 5.1.14 . . . 63

Jerome
Illustrious Men 2 11

III. The Rabbis and Related Sources

Mishnah

Berakoth 2.1 44
Terumoth 8.12........... 79 ff.
Sheqalim 1.3 f........... 42 ff.
           1.4 44
           1.6 44
Nedarim 3.4............... 53
Sotah 9.9 30
Qiddushin 1.1 60
Baba Qamma 8.1 21
              8.6 21
Niddah 5.4................ 60

Tosephta

Terumoth 7.20........... 79 ff.
Erubin 4.7 46
Pesahim 1.27 51

Jerusalemite Talmud

Berakoth 4b............... 44
Kilaim 32c 73
Shebiith 38d .... 113 f.
Terumoth 46b .... 79 ff.
Megillah 71c 2
Yebamoth 12a............. 60
Gittin 48c................. 23
Sanhedrin 21b 82
Abodah Zarah 40a......... 51

Babylonian Talmud

Berakoth 13b f. 44
            19a 44
Shabbath 33b ff........ 85, 100,
                     112, 114
            113b............ 33
Erubin 64b............... 51
Pesahim 112a.......... 85, 112
Yoma 19a f................ 45
Taanith 2a................ 8
Megillah 13b 66

Yebamoth 22a............. 60
           48b......... 60, 65 f.
           62a............. 60
           68b 42
           98b 60
Nedarim 28a 53
           35b 45
Qiddushin 23b............ 45
           77a ff........... 60
Sanhedrin 58a ff. 60
           70b 25
           74a 82
           90b........... 4, 5
Abodah Zarah 6a.......... 49
Menahoth 21b f. 44
           46b 44
Arakin 4a 44

Mekhilta on Exodus

12.40.................... 17
16.35.................... 73
21.35.................... 20

Siphre on Numbers

5.31..................... 30
12.12.................... 71

Siphre on Deuteronomy

11.21................... 114

Tannaim on Deuteronomy

25.11.................... 21

Genesis Rabba

1.26 f. 17
6.9...................... 28, 67
12.2..................... 60
24.13................... 109
29.22.................... 36
38.1.................... 90, 95

39.7 34
46.26 f. . . . . 79 ff., 87

Exodus Rabba
32.7 . . . . 90, 95

Leviticus Rabba
27.2 51

Numbers Rabba
4.19 66

Deuteronomy Rabba
10.1 31

Ruth Rabba
1.16 66
1.18 66
2.14 33

Pirqe de-Rabbi Eliezer
38 98

Zadokite Fragments
7.1 ff. 18 f.

I Qumran Hodayoth
6.29 f. 9
6.34 9

Prayer-Book 6, 7, 8, 12, 13,
16, 40, 41, 52, 57

Philo
On the Creation 24.76 (17) . . . 17
*Allegorical Interpretation of the
Laws* 1.24.76 (59) 70
2.4.13 (69) 17

On Drunkenness 4.14 (359) . . . 24
6.22 (360) . . . 24
7.25 (361) . . . 25
Who Is the Heir
33.164 (496) 17
On the Change of Names
37.206 (609) 24
On Abraham 7.36 ff. (7) 28
The Special Laws
2.41.232 (298) 26
Embassy to Gaius
32.229 ff. (580) 86

Pseudo-Philo
Antiquities 21 A 73

Josephus
Life 2.9 115
Against Apion 2.8.106 48
Jewish War 2.14.8.301 ff. 80
7.6.6.218 53
Jewish Antiquities
2.3.3.15 116
2.3.4.38 97
2.7.1.186 f. 98
3.10.7.255 45
5.7.10.263 f. 109
7.11.8.291 . . . . 79, 104
12.6.2.276 f. 46
12.10.1.389 ff. 87
13.1.3.12 f. 46
18.5.2.117 ff. 89
20.2.4.38 ff. 65

IV. Classical Sources

Aeschylus
Agamemnon 1624 68
Suppliant Maidens 105

Aristotle
Art of Rhetoric
2.23.16.1399a 31

Aristotle (*continued*)
  Sophistical Refutations
    2.12.173a 31

Dio Cassius
  Roman History Epit. 65.7.2. . . 53

Euripides
  Bacchanals 795 68
  The Children of Hercules
    543 ff. 101

Herodotus
  Histories 1.114 ff. 115
              3.119 42

Philostratus
  The Life of Apollonius of Tyana
    1.7. 115
    8.12. 16

Pindar
  Pythian Odes 2.95. 68

Plato
  Symposium 189C ff. 18

Plutarch
  Parallel Lives,
    Alexander 5.1 115

    Pelopidas 21.1 106
    Theseus 15.1 108

Anonymous
  Ad Herennium 2.24.38. 31

Cicero
  Pro Ligario 11.35 103

Digest
  9.2.27.5 (Ulpian XVIII
    ad edictum) 20
  46.3.67 (Marcellus XIII
    digestorum) 49

Festus
  Signification of Words,
    Paul's Excerpts 379 106

Livy
  From the Founding of the City
    9.46.7 ff. 86
    33.52.4 45

Suetonius
  Lives of the Caesars,
    Domitian 12.2 53

Tacitus
  Histories 5.5 63

Compositor:	G & S Typesetters, Inc.
Text:	10/12 Bembo
Display:	Bembo
Printer:	Thomson–Shore, Inc.
Binder:	John H. Dekker & Sons, Inc.